SOVEREIGN SOUL CONVERSATIONS

A Blueprint for Transforming Your Reality and Securing Your Peace

Lesley Morgan Jenkins

WP PRESS LLC

CONTENTS

DEDICATION

To my sons:

May you be such men of honor, and may you love so well, that the women in your lives never have to open a book like this.

Introduction

Let Me Put The Kettle On

Come on in and take a seat. Girl, make yourself comfortable. Where's my hug? Because we all know a big hug means that it's going to be alright. Take those shoes off, put your feet up on the sofa. Here's a blanket and a soft pillow for your back. You hungry? You want some coffee or tea? I knew you would—I'll put the kettle on.

Chances are you've experienced this scene before in more ways than one, either with you being the safe haven or being the one in search of peace. This is the mark of womanhood and sisterhood—the love and peace that comes from a sip of a hot cup in good company.

So take a minute to get yourself settled in, because in this place of peace and calm also comes some gentle confrontation and some raw truths—laughter, too. But we're about to get to work, because the truth is: you are too amazing, too wonderful, and too full of life and promise to be stuck behind this cup of coffee.

Life may be messy right now. Things don't make sense. You may have just experienced the biggest blow that you've ever had to face, or maybe you're in a place where you can finally take a minute to process what in the world just happened and how to heal and move forward.

I can't say that I have all the answers for you, but Sis, I'm here. Me and this cup of coffee. Together, we're going to walk through this life of yours like it's a house that's been through a few storms. We're going to look past the peeling paint and the flickering lights, and we're going to start exactly where we need to: by proving that your foundation is still standing.

Let's head down to the basement and check the bones of this place.

1

THE FOUNDATION IS SOLID

YOU ARE STRUCTURALLY SOUND

Now that you've got your cup and your feet are up, I need to ask you a favor. I need you to put down the *I'm a disaster* song for just a second. I know, it's comfortable. It's the old, oversized sweater you wear when you're hiding. But we're doing a home inspection today, and we need all things to be revealed. And honey, that sweater is getting in the way of the truth.

When a house has been through a hurricane, the first thing people check isn't the curtains or the flower beds. They go straight to the basement. They check the foundation. Because if the foundation is cracked, nothing else matters—but if the foundation is solid, the house can be rebuilt.

Sis, your foundation is more than solid. It's reinforced steel.

The fact that you are still standing, regardless of the tears or how weak you may feel, is proof that you are reinforced steel. Let me say that again so that you hear it: *You are standing!* After the heartbreak; after the dream job cut you; the one you just knew was *the one* left you; the loss of a parent or of your own child—whatever it is. The simple fact that you have not lost your mind or taken your own life, that you got up out of the bed, no matter how difficult it was, is all proof that you are, in fact, strong. You may not have washed yourself today (but who does that every day anyway?). You may be in the same comfy pjs you had on two days ago, and that's okay—you are here! So let's start by celebrating that.

Then we're going to celebrate the fact that you had enough strength to call for help. Because asking for help is most certainly not a sign of weakness. No Sis—it is a form of strength and humanity. It's what makes our bonds of sisterhood so strong—there is peace in knowing that you can cry on my shoulder or show up at my door with your face unwashed and snotty and still receive that hug and that mug and know that someone is in your corner.

So before we talk about how you feel, let's talk about the facts. You have a 100% survival rate for every single worst day of your life. Every heartbreak, every *I can't do this anymore* moment, every time the rug was pulled out from under you and the times where you can barely breathe—you're still here. That's not luck.

That's structural integrity.

But before we keep digging into the basement, I need you to understand one thing: You own the land. See, the world likes to tell us our value depends on how pretty the curtains look or if the lawn is mowed—basically, how well we're *performing*. But your worth isn't something you earned with a promotion or lost in a breakup. It's the Title Deed to your soul. It's the original paperwork that was signed before you ever even moved in. It says that even if the roof is leaking and the porch is sagging, the value of the property hasn't changed. You don't have to *fix* the house to be worthy of living in it. You are the rightful owner simply because you are you. So while we're working on the repairs, don't you dare think that a few cracked windows mean the house is condemned. Your value is built into the ground you stand on.

Take a minute and think about all the other things you've already overcome. You bounced back from the last heartache. You learned from the last betrayal. When you lost your job, you got up and got another one—it may not have been exactly what you wanted, but it paid the bills. The days and nights may have felt endless, but because you went through the process, you came out stronger, more purpose-driven, more you on the other side.

And what's more—you healed. What about the last time you

scraped your knee or cut your finger? You didn't have to tell your body what to do. Your cells didn't have a meeting to decide if you were worthy of healing. They just got to work. Your skin knit itself back together. Your bones, when they break, grow back stronger at the point of the fracture.

You come from a long line of women who survived slavery, abuse, famine, and heartaches you can't even imagine. Their resilience is literally written into your DNA. You aren't just trying to be strong; you are built of strength. Say it out loud, with your chest; write it on every mirror you have:

"I am built of strength!"

I don't want to take away from anything that you're feeling right now, because your emotions are real and they are valid, so please, take the time to feel and to process them. Scream, cry, yell, ask why, be numb, be angry, feel broken or bitter. Let's laugh about the good times and mourn what could have been. The more you bring yourself to express it, the more you're clearing the debris.

And just like a deep home renovation, there are layers to this work. Some days you'll be stripping back old wallpaper and find a message written on the drywall that gives you a whole new perspective. Other days, you'll be scrubbing a floor and it'll feel like the grime is never coming up—and that's okay. It's all part of the restoration, Sis. Some days the dust is going to kick up and make it hard to breathe, and other days you'll finally see the sun hitting a corner of the room you thought was gone for good. Just remember, this is a no-judgment zone, because I'm sitting here in the dust and the process with you, too.

Even when you're in the thick of that renovation, there is unstoppable movement on the inside of you. Your resilience is that backup generator that keeps humming, even when the power grid is out. Let's continue our home inspection of your resilience.

When a storm is howling outside, good windows keep the noise out so you can hear the conversation inside. Resilience is your ability to filter the noise—the panic, the gossip, the self-doubt—so you can focus on the signal: the next step.

Think of this as your internal architect. When you're mid-renovation and you tear down a wall only to find an unexpected pipe right where you wanted to put a door, you don't burn the house down. You don't just stop and freeze, no! You just adjust the blueprint. Resilience is treating your mistakes like a floor plan adjustment. "Oops, that path is blocked. Recalculating... okay, the new door goes here." It's a shift in the design, not confirmation that you are a total disaster.

A resilient system can switch from high to low power modes

without crashing. You've done this. You've survived the big power outages of life because your internal backup generator kicked in. You kept breathing. You kept showing up. And you will continue to. Why?

Because you are built of strength.

One thing I know, regardless of how you deal with it, life will move on with or without you. You've seen the inspection report. Your foundation is steel, your history is proof, and your system is working. So now you have to choose whether or not you're going to get stuck here in the basement, or if you're willing to do something different to push through. Your house, however storm-torn, is standing. So what are you going to do?

The coffee is hot. Let's get to work.

2

THROWING OUT THE USELESS CLUTTER

CLEARING THE JOB SITE

Alright! Now that we know the bones of this house are solid, we need to talk about why you've been tripping over your own feet lately. It's the clutter, Sis. Not the physical kind—though I'm sure that chair in your bedroom has a pile of clothes on it, no shade—but I'm talking about the mental kind. The worst kind of clutter is the stuff we've been holding onto because we're too ashamed to throw it away. We think if we keep it hidden in the back of the closet, it's not there, but it's taking up space.

It's the *monster under the bed*—we all have one—that voice that waits until the house is quiet and you're finally trying to rest to start whispering all the reasons why you aren't enough. It's that inner voice that tells you every mistake you've ever made is a permanent stain on the carpet and replays them over and over again in your mind at all hours. The dark inner dialogue that keeps peeking out from the shadows and going bump in the night. It's the *vicious beast* of your mind that feeds on your hesitation, trying to grow big enough to block the doorway to your future.

It's like an illegal tenant that moved into your guest room and refuses to leave. He's eating your food, making a mess of your thoughts, and trying to convince you he owns the place. But honey, he's just a squatter. You have the deed. He's the *vicious beast* of your mind that feeds on your hesitation, trying to grow big enough to block the doorway to your future.

We're moving from the basement up to the main hallway and the closets. It's time to start tossing the junk that's making the house feel small, crowded, and cluttered. But before we start dragging the big boxes out, I want us to take the shame out of this conversation entirely. You're in my living room right now, and girl, trust me, I've been trying to think of a way to discreetly pick up the toys and shoes that my kids just left out last night. I know you see them, too—don't judge me! We're both human.

Shame is the *black mold of the soul*; it grows in the dark and makes the whole house toxic. If we can take the shame out of the mistake, we can treat our past failures like a bad paint choice—something we can just prime and paint over with a better color.

In a renovation, there is always a mess. There are buckets of who knows what—nails, power tools, and sawdust everywhere. Sometimes, you cut a piece of wood too short. When that happens, you don't call yourself a failure of a builder. You don't sit in the sawdust and cry that you'll never have a kitchen. You just say, "Well, that piece is too short," and you go get a new board. That is taking the shame out of the mistake. A mistake is just a piece of data. It's feedback. It's the house telling you, "Hey, that plumbing doesn't work that way, try again." It has no bearing on your worth—it's not calling you stupid, incompetent, unworthy, incapable, or any of the other million negative things that start rushing through our heads and turn our cheeks hot and make us want to run and hide. We do that to ourselves.

And I get it, Sis, because that inner dialogue came from somewhere; we all have it in some shape or form. But just like you had the choice to come out of the basement and keep reading into Chapter 2, you can make a choice to turn on the lights and tell that inner monster to "have several seats" while you keep on pushing forward. It's going to take some effort on your part to hear it, acknowledge it, and then choose to turn the light on and ignore the noise. When you stop seeing mistakes as a reflection of your worth and start seeing them as design feedback, you become unstoppable. You can't fix a house if you're too ashamed to admit the roof is leaking because you're scared of what's hiding in the attic.

So, how do we actually tell that voice to sit down and hush? First, you have to learn to *catch the creak.* You know how when a house is settling, you hear a pop or a groan in the hallway? You don't panic and think the roof is falling in; you just recognize, *Oh, that's just the house settling.* That's the first tip: Call it out by name. When that voice says you're a failure, stop and say, "That's just the *mind monster* again." By naming it, you stop being in the feeling and start being the person watching the feeling.

Next, you've got to separate the data from the drama. If the roof is leaking, the data is simply: *there is water in the living room.* The drama is: *I am a terrible homeowner, I'll never be able to afford this, and I'm a mess for letting this happen.* Deleting the noise means you grab the data—the fact that something needs to be fixed—and you toss the drama out the window. Ask yourself, "What is the one objective fact here?" If you missed a deadline, the fact is the deadline was missed. That's it. Everything else is just static.

Finally, I want you to carry a mantra around with you like a tape measure in your pocket. Every time you trip over a mistake and that shame starts to rise up, I want you to say this out loud: *"This is data for my blueprint, not a stain on my soul."* Say it until you believe it. Because the more you practice extracting the lesson without the lecture, the faster this renovation is going to go. You're not a bad builder because you hit a snag; you're a smart builder because you're willing to adjust the plan and keep the hammers swinging.

Do you need a second cup? Mine is getting low, so I'm going to pause real quick and grab some more. I can whip us up something to eat if you'd like.

Alright, so let's look at these leaky lies together.

I. The Leaky Lies

The Imposter The first box of junk we're dragging to the curb is that *Imposter* lie—that nagging feeling that you're just a squatter in your own life and any minute now, someone is going to realize you don't belong here. Sis! You bought this house! You own the deed. You belong here exactly as you are, snotty nose and all. Are you really going to let someone else make you feel uncomfortable in the house you own? No ma'am! So let's kick this lie to the curb and call Tyrone to come get him. Your life is as beautiful as you have made it. If you don't like it, then change it. If there's something you want to learn, then let's work on gaining that knowledge, because you can put your mind to anything you want to achieve. But here's the truth: anywhere and everywhere that you find yourself is exactly where you are supposed to be. You have earned every penny of it. You have the scars and the wisdom to show for it. I say wisdom, because education is not always found in books, and just because someone is book smart, doesn't mean they know how to apply it. So apply it honey, like the boss you are, and bask in the glory of your capabilities.

Too Late Right next to that is the *Too Late* lie. This is the shame of wasted years, the feeling that the best time to renovate was a decade ago and now it's just not worth the effort. But the best time to fix a roof is the day you realize it's leaking. The clock doesn't matter; the shelter does. Your timeline isn't a failure; it's just your story. What's our mantra again? *"This is data for my blueprint, not a stain on my soul."* You are still here, which means that there is still time—so get to work! And I'll add this extra nugget for you to consider. Even if you had renovated 10 years ago, you'd probably be ready for an upgrade now anyway. Think about how much more you've learned in the time that's elapsed—that's just more for you to have to offer now. So get those hips moving, and do it now!

What Will The Neighbors Think? Then there's that heavy box labeled *What Will the Neighbors Think?* Don't even get me started on this one! We spend so much time worrying about people looking at our unfinished siding that we stop working on the inside. But those neighbors aren't living in your house; you are. Their opinion doesn't keep the rain out, and it definitely won't help you finish the floors. Quite frankly, those neighbors may actually benefit from you finishing your renovation work quickly and may even compliment you for the upgrades. Hey, who knows if they'll start working on their own? What if the neighbors think that your idea is so amazing that they want to help you finish the build? What if your neighbor is the exact person to help you launch into your next? What if? Baby let them stare, let them gawk, let them laugh or side eye, it's ok. The truth is, they probably aren't as focused on you as you think they are, so worrying about them is only stopping you from moving forward for yourself.

Already Been Done We also have to toss the lie that it's *Already Been Done.* You might think your dreams aren't worth pursuing because someone else already did it. Honey, there are a million white kitchens in the world, but this one is yours. Your touch, your flavor, and your life are what make it new, interesting and unique. And again, this is your house; the one you live in, so you need to be happy and comfortable in it. They may have the same floor plan, but they don't have your paint palette. Your unique perspective is the color that makes this house a home. Don't worry about the neighbors' neutral beige; you paint your walls the color of your joy. I'll just throw this one in there for free—sometimes the remake is better than the original—I'm thinking Kelly Price vs. Shirley Murdock, Keke Wyatt vs. Patti Labelle, Donell Jones vs. Stevie Wonder... ok, ok, musical beauty is in the ear of the beholder. But that's actually kind of my point. Both the original and the remakes have their own special qualities, so what really matters is which one you prefer.

What If I Fail? Finally, we have to face the big one: the *What If I Fail?* lie. This is the fear that a single mistake equals a total collapse. But remember the renovation change we talked about? A mistake is just a change in the floor plan—a smart reroute. It's a shift in the design, not a disaster. Let's be brutally honest—you're never going to be perfect 100% of the time—and that is okay—it's what makes you human. Failure is only a problem if you allow it to keep you stuck. You can always readjust and try again. Maybe what you should be asking is: what if you fly?

The Shouldas As we clear these rooms, we have to throw out the *Shouldas*, too. Those are like the glossy home magazines we keep around that make us feel bad about our real, lived-in lives. "I should have been further along," or "I should have seen that coming." *Should* is just shame in a fancy dress, and it has no place in this renovation. We're working with the house we have, not the one a magazine showed us. Your perceived deficits do not define you, they are not limiting factors of you, in fact, they are the keys to unlocking your superpowers. The question is: will you allow them to stop you from reaching your potential?

Renovation Work Orders: Hauling the Junk

The Deed Review: If you feel like an *Imposter*, check your paperwork. Start a receipts folder. Every thank-you note, every "you crushed that" email, and every memory of a time you survived the impossible goes in there. When that squatter feeling creeps in, read your receipts. You didn't stumble into this life; you paid for it in grit, grind and grace.

The Upgrade Audit: To silence the *Too Late* lie, draw a line down a piece of paper. On the left, write *Me 10 Years Ago*. On the right, write *Me Today*. List three things you know now—the wisdom, the survival skills, the street smarts, the perspective—that you didn't have then. You'll see that the version of you from a decade ago couldn't have handled this level of renovation. Today, you are the only one qualified for the job.

The Frosted Glass Method: If you can't stop looking at the neighbors, change the view. Identify your digital neighbors—the social media accounts that make you feel like your siding isn't good enough—and mute them for 30 days. If your neighbor is analog, then avoid or decrease your interaction with them as much as possible. You need to focus on your own self, your own family and your own floors, and you can't do that if you're staring out the window at someone else's lawn.

The Signature Sauce Test: Remind yourself that there are a million chili recipes, but none have your exact seasoning. Take one goal you have and identify your signature ingredient. Is it your humor? Your honesty? Write that one word down and tape it to your mirror. When you see someone else doing your idea, tell yourself: "They may have the kitchen, but they don't have my sauce."

The Controlled Demo: Stop fearing the collapse by realizing how easy it is to patch a hole. Do something small this week that you are intentionally bad at—a new hobby or a difficult recipe. When you mess it up, look around. The sun still rose, the coffee was still hot, and your house didn't fall down. You're practicing the smart reroute. If you can, document your journey so that you can see your own improvements over time.

Speak It Out Loud:

I am clearing the floor so I can build my future.

II. The Air is Clearing

Once you've hauled those five boxes to the curb and finished your work orders, I want you to take a deep breath. Can you feel the difference? Remember, shame is the black mold of the soul. It grows in the dark, damp corners of our secrets and our "should-haves," and if you leave it alone, it eventually makes the whole house toxic. It makes you think the structure is rotting when really, it's just a surface mess that needs some air. By dragging these lies out into the front yard, you've just hit that mold with a heavy dose of bleach and sunlight.

But listen to me, Sis—getting rid of mold is a process, especially if it's been sitting in the walls for a while. You might scrub one corner today only to find a little bit more peeking through next week. That doesn't mean you failed; it just means the roots were deep. You may need to keep coming back to this conversation, keep rereading these truths, and keep applying that bleach as a form of mold remediation for your mind. Don't get discouraged if the mind monster tries to settle back in. Just open the windows again. The musty feeling of not enough is finally lifting, and for the first time in a long time, you can actually see the potential in these rooms. The air is fresh. Now that we've cleared the space, let's see what's left to work with.

3

TAKING INVENTORY

WHAT'S IN THE JUNK DRAWER?

Oh! The food's ready! Let's take this conversation into the kitchen. C'mon, grab your cup.

Moving into the kitchen feels different, you know? It's the heart of the home, the place where we nourish ourselves—mind, body and soul—but it's also where the real work gets done. Now that we've hauled the junk to the curb and told that *mind monster* where to go, the house probably feels a little empty. I know that emptiness sometimes feels heavy, but I want you to look at it differently—empty is just another word for room to grow. Before we go out and try to buy a whole new life or look for external solutions to internal problems, we need to see what's already in these cabinets.

I want you to walk with me over to the counter. Set your mug down for a second and let's open that one drawer—you know exactly which one I'm talking about. Every house has one. It's the junk drawer. At first glance, it's a bit of a mess—you've got mismatched batteries, a half-roll of duct tape, a stray screwdriver, and a handful of spare keys you aren't even sure go to anything anymore. To an outsider, it looks like a junk pile, but to a woman on a mission, that drawer is a goldmine. It's where the solutions live. And honey, you are full of solutions whether you believe it or not.

When we go through a crisis, we often feel bankrupt, like the storm took everything of value. But Sis, you have a set of tools in your junk drawer that you've been taking for granted because they've just become part of the background noise. I want you to look at those leftover skills you've spent a lifetime perfecting. Maybe your tool is resourcefulness—that incredible ability to make a gourmet meal out of two cans of beans and a prayer. That's not just getting by, honey; that's high-level creativity and project management. Maybe your tool is discernment, that quiet gut feeling that acts like a level, telling you exactly when something is leaning the wrong way. Or maybe it's pure grit—the heavy-duty screwdriver that keeps your life (and everyone else's) together when all the other screws are coming loose.

Don't look at these as scraps! These are your primary building materials. You don't need a fancy, professional contractor's kit to start fixing your life; you just need to realize that the tape and the mismatched batteries you've collected through your survival years are exactly what's required for this stage of the build.

Here's the crazy thing about it: these probably don't even look or feel like tools to you, because you do them with such ease. But trust me, not everyone can swing that hammer like you can, and because of that, it is a superpower.

While we're standing here, let's take a hard look at the pantry, too. You cannot expect to pull twelve-hour shifts on a renovation if you're trying to survive on crumbs of regret and *mind monster* leftovers. What are you feeding your mind right now? If your internal pantry is stocked with doom-scrolling, toxic news, and conversations with people who only want to talk about how bad the hurricane was, you're going to run out of fuel before the first board is nailed down. We have to restock. We need some good soul food—the kind of sustenance that actually supports the work. That means being greedy with your peace, seeking out high-quality silence, and choosing a diet of thoughts and voices that remind you of your power rather than your pain.

Finally, let's talk about those spare keys rattling around in the bottom of the drawer. A house is a lot easier to fix when you aren't the only one with a key, but you have to be careful about who you let in while the walls are open. Part of taking inventory is realizing who truly belongs in this house and who needs to have their access revoked. Some people are *demo-crew*—they are fantastic at helping you tear things down and vent about the past, but they have no idea how to help you build a future. Other people are *architects*—they see the vision of who you're becoming even when you're standing in a pile of sawdust. Look at your inner circle. Who can you call when the plumbing bursts at 3 AM? If that list is short, don't panic. A small, solid crew that knows how to hold a hammer is a thousand times better than a house full of people who are just there for the party and disappear the moment the work starts.

You have more than what you think you have, but you can't see it because you haven't taken the time to organize the drawer. So let's start now. You are well-equipped, Sis. You've got everything you need to start the rebuild.

I. Digging Deeper into the Drawer

I've given you a few examples of the tools I see in you, but I know your drawer is deeper than that. There are things in there that only you know how to use—tools you forged in fires I haven't walked through. Sometimes we don't recognize our own superpowers because we've had to use them for so long that they feel like a second skin. But Sis, common sense isn't always common, and the way you've navigated your life is proof of a high-level skill set that not everyone is blessed to have.

To help you find the tools I know I missed, I want you to sit with that drawer open and ask yourself these three questions:

- **What is the thing people always come to me for?** Are you the one they call when a situation is spiraling and they need a calm in the storm? That's the tool of emotional regulation and crisis management. Are you the one they call when they need the ugly truth wrapped in love? That's integrity. Whatever your phone-a-friend reason is, that's a power tool.

- **What have I survived that should have broken me, and how did I do it?** When the *mind monster* was loudest and the walls felt like they were closing in, what was the one thing that kept you standing? Was it your ability to pivot? Was it your silence? Was it your stubborn refusal to be defeated? That *how* is a tool you can use to build your new kitchen.

- **What do I do so effortlessly that I forget other people struggle with it?** Maybe you can organize a chaotic schedule in your head, or you can read a room the second you walk through the door. Because it's easy for you, you think it's nothing. It's not nothing—it's an advanced leveling tool.

II. The Vouch: Owning the Assignment

Before we start swinging hammers, we have to talk about who actually has the final say in this house. You can look at the tools in your drawer and see your own strength, but if you're still waiting for the world to vouch for you, you'll never actually pick up the hammer.

We've all seen HGTV so you know how it works in a real renovation—the inspector has to come by, look at the work, and sign off on the permit before you can move to the next stage. A lot of us are living our lives in a permanent waiting period. We're waiting for a parent, an ex-partner, a boss, or even society to walk through our halls, nod their head, and say, *Okay, you're qualified to be happy now. You've paid enough to prove yourself. You're actually good at this.*

Hear me carefully: Sis, that inspector isn't coming. And even if they did, they don't live here, you do! Why are you letting someone who doesn't know the layout of your heart decide if your build is valid?

Sis, that permit was signed the day you were created. Vouching for yourself isn't about being arrogant or self-made. It's actually about Divine alignment. It's about looking at your life and saying, *If the One who made me hasn't given up on me, then I don't have the right to give up on myself.*

Vouching for yourself means you stop asking for permission to be the expert on your own life. It means when that *mind monster* whispers that you're unqualified, you don't look for a second opinion—you look at your own track record. You vouch for your own character. You vouch for your own resilience. You look at that snotty-nosed, scarred-up, hair still tied up in a scarf woman in the mirror and you say, *I know her. I've seen what she can do in the dark. I trust her to build in the light.*

When you vouch for yourself, you're simply agreeing with the Master Architect. You're acknowledging that you were built with a purpose, and that every tool in your utility drawer was placed there by design—not by accident. You don't need to be perfect to be authorized. You just need to be willing to work with what you've been given—and honey, you have been given a whole lot, because all of heaven is backing you!

III. The Vouching Audit

If you're struggling to vouch for yourself, I want you to be a witness to your own life. Ask yourself:

- **Who am I waiting for an apology or approval from?** Write that name down, then draw a big X over it. They don't hold the permit for your future. Choose to forgive them, choose to let it go. If you have to keep saying it over and over again until it's real—then do it! This is for you! It has absolutely nothing to do with them.

- **What is one win I've had that I've been calling luck?** Stop it. Luck didn't get you through that storm; you did. Own that win! Being humble does not mean that we demean or diminish ourselves. You can be quietly confident, but the key word is confidence!

- **If my best friend was standing in this exact house, would I vouch for her?** Of course you would. You'd tell her she's a boss. Now, why is your vouch for her stronger than your vouch for yourself?

Renovation Work Orders: The Inventory Check

This week, I want you to actually organize the drawer of your mind.

The Tool Inventory: Identify your three power tools—these are natural skills like your budget-savviness, your loyalty, or your ability to learn on the fly—and acknowledge them as the assets they are. Acknowledging that you're a good mother, a hard worker, or a loyal friend isn't bragging—it's just an honest inventory of the resources in your hands.

The Pantry Purge: Look at your screen time or your circle. If a certain social media feed or a certain friend makes you feel like your house is beyond repair, toss them. Find one thing that actually feeds your strength and spend twenty minutes there every day.

The Key Audit: Look at the people you spend the most time with. Do they help you build, or do they just leave muddy footprints on your clean floors? You don't have to kick everyone out today, but you do need to decide who gets to keep their spare key and who only gets to visit when the porch light is on.

Speak it Out Loud:

I am a work in progress, but I am already a masterpiece. I don't need a signature from the world to move forward. I trust the tools I've been given, I trust the strength I've been shown, and I vouch for the woman I am becoming.

4

DRAFTING THE BLUEPRINT

DESIGNING YOUR "NEXT"

Woo child! That was heavy, but it's alright. That's why you came over here—for a hug, some coffee and some real talk! And I fed you, too. Let's see what we have for dessert while we really start to dig into this. Grab a slice of this cake while we look at the drawings. You can't plan a whole new wing on an empty stomach!

I know what you're saying to me. You're saying, "Girl, I know all of this. I've gone to counseling, I've been praying and meditating, I've been journaling, and I've been working on myself. I've been doing this for a while, and it just feels like I keep getting stuck in some places."

I hear you. And I applaud you for the work you've put in. But just like in a home, there's always going to be something popping up that needs attention—it's home maintenance. Just like you do your hair and your nails every two weeks, you still have to maintain. Sometimes that maintenance is a bit more involved. You don't stop sweeping the floors just because you deep-cleaned them last month; you keep the broom handy because life keeps moving in.

But here is the underlying issue with being stuck: oftentimes we try to maintain a house we don't actually like. We spend all our energy maintaining a life that was designed by someone else's expectations or our own past mistakes. It's hard to keep cleaning up a room you never wanted to be in anyway. That's why, before we pick up the broom again, we need to look at the *Blueprint*.

I. The Standard Floor Plan Trap

The reason the maintenance feels so heavy is that you might be trying to maintain a *Standard Floor Plan* that no longer fits who you are today. We've all been handed a plan at some point—maybe it was from your parents, your culture, or even a version of yourself that doesn't exist anymore.

If the layout of your life is causing you to trip over the same obstacles every two weeks, it's not just a maintenance problem; it's a design flaw. You're working twice as hard to keep up a lifestyle or a mindset that was never meant for you. It's time to move the walls. It's time to take yourself back to that little girl who dreamt big before anyone told her that she couldn't. I know it's in you somewhere, and because we've been cleaning up that cobwebby basement and pulling all the junk out of those closets, it's probably closer to your mind than you think. Before you draw a single line on your new blueprint, ask yourself: "Is this room here because I want it, or because I was told I needed it?"

II. Designing for the Current Season

A house that worked for you ten years ago might not work for you now. In a real home, your needs change. Maybe you needed a playroom back then, but now you need an office. Maybe you needed a big table for entertaining, but now you need a quiet corner for your peace.

If you feel stuck, it might be because you're trying to maintain a version of your life that has already expired. You're scrubbing the floors of a past season instead of prepping the foundation for what's coming next. Drafting a blueprint isn't about being ungrateful for where you've been; it's about being honest about where you're going. Even if you aren't ready to build the new wing yet, you need to know where the doors are going to be.

III. The Non-Negotiable Pillars

In every blueprint, there are certain things that are structural—the pillars that keep the roof from caving in. As we look at your new design, we have to identify your non-negotiables.

If your home maintenance keeps failing because you're sacrificing your peace, your health, or your boundaries to keep everyone else happy, you've got a structural issue. Your pillars are leaning. We're going to set those straight first. These are the parts of the house we do not compromise on. Everything else—the paint colors, the extra rooms, the nice-to-haves—can be shifted, but the pillars stay put.

In a house, a pillar is a load-bearing vertical support. It's not a decoration; it's what keeps the ceiling from becoming the floor. For example, that weird column in the kitchen that attaches to the island and kind of gets in the way of your aesthetic—but you know you can't move it or your upstairs master bathroom would end up in your kitchen. Yes, that's the one I'm talking about. In your life, a pillar is a core value that you've decided is non-negotiable. It's a boundary that defines who you are and who you belong to—your family, your purpose, and the original design the Architect had for you before the world got its hands on you.

Understand, when I say *Pillar*, I'm not talking about a New Year's Resolution or a goal like losing weight or saving money. I'm talking about the structural values that support your soul. If you build a room in your life—a new job, a new relationship, or a new commitment—and it doesn't fit around your pillars, that room is going to cause a collapse eventually.

Examples of Pillars in Action:

- **The Pillar of Peace:** This means you have decided that your mental and emotional well-being is a requirement, not a luxury. If a new opportunity comes along that pays more but requires you to live in a state of constant anxiety and chaos, it doesn't fit. You don't move the pillar to fit the room; you reject the room because it won't fit the house.

- **The Pillar of Integrity:** This is your *True North.* It means that being honest and staying true to your word is more important than being liked or getting ahead. If a situation requires you to shave off a bit of your truth to make it work, you realize that's a structural failure. You can't build on a lie.

- **The Pillar of Presence:** Maybe for you, being present for your children or your own self-care is a load-bearer. If a good thing starts taking you away from the best things, your house is going to feel hollow.

- **Why They Must Be at the Top of Your Paper** Imagine you're building a kitchen. You can't just put the stove wherever you want if there's a massive structural pillar in the way. You have to design the kitchen around that pillar. When you write your three pillars in bold at the top of your paper, you are saying: "Whatever I plan next—whether it's how I spend my Saturdays, who I date, or how I talk to myself—it has to respect these three things. If a commitment tries to knock down my Pillar of Peace, then that commitment doesn't get a seat at my table."

How to Find Your Pillars If you're struggling to name your pillars, ask yourself:

1. What is the one thing that, if I lost it, I wouldn't recognize myself anymore? (That's a pillar).

2. What have I sacrificed in the past that left me feeling 'homeless' inside? (That's a pillar you forgot to protect).

3. What do I want to be known for when I'm 80 years old? (That's a pillar you're building toward).

Renovation Work Orders: Drafting Your Next

Since we're sitting here with dessert, let's get a fresh piece of paper and start sketching.

The Pillar Check: List three things you will no longer negotiate away. Write them in **bold** at the top of your paper. Every new room or commitment you add to your life has to fit around these three pillars.

The *What's Not Working* Audit: Identify one area of your life where maintenance feels like an uphill battle. Is it a specific habit? A lopsided relationship? A job that drains you? Ask yourself: Is this hard because I'm not trying, or is it hard because this room doesn't belong in my house anymore?

The Atmosphere Vision: Close your eyes and imagine yourself a year from now, walking through your front door. Don't look at the furniture—look at the feeling. Is it quiet? Is it stable? Is it vibrant? If you can identify the atmosphere you want, we can start building the walls to hold it.

The Project Plan: Fix, Replace, or Remove? When a contractor looks at a room that isn't working, they categorize the work into three levels of action:

Fix (F): This is your creaky door—it works fine, it's just out of alignment. You don't need a sledgehammer; you need a wrench. You tighten a boundary or set a new habit.

Replace (R): Think of an outdated bathroom—it's still valuable and needed, but it needs an upgrade to fit your new life. You change the terms of a relationship or a job or activity.

Remove/Gut (G): This thing has to go! It's rotted through, stinking up the place, and if it stays much longer, it's going to cause damage to the things around it. This is a toxic mindset or situation. It needs a total teardown before you can lay something new.

Strengthening the Foundation: Pillar Actions

The Fix-Up: *The Re-Alignment* If your pillar is crooked, it means you've drifted. You still believe in the value, but your daily actions aren't lining up with it anymore.

The Action: Execute one *Strategic No.* Look at your calendar for the next seven days. Find one thing you said yes to out of habit, guilt, or *shouldas* that directly conflicts with your pillar of Rest or Peace. Cancel it. One *No* to the world is often a *Yes* to your own foundation. And remember, *No* is a complete sentence.

The Replacement: *The External Brace* When a pillar is being crushed by too much weight, you don't necessarily move the pillar; you bring in extra support so it doesn't have to carry the load alone.

The Action: Automate or Delegate one Burden. If your pillar of *Family Presence* is being crushed by the weight of household chores or work emails, you install a brace. This might mean setting an auto-reply on your email after 6:00 PM or finally telling your kids or partner that they are now in charge of their own laundry.

The Removal/Gut Job: *The Identity Swap* This is the hardest work. This is when you realize that what you thought was a support beam is actually a rotted-out post. You've been building your life on *Being Liked* (People Pleasing) and calling it *Being a Good Person* (Kindness). Throw it out like a bad habit!

The Action: Perform a *Motive Check* before your next yes. The next time someone asks you for a favor or a commitment, wait ten seconds. Ask yourself: "Am I doing this because it aligns with my values, or because I'm afraid they'll be mad if I don't?" If the answer is fear, you refuse the request.

Changing What No Longer Serves Me

The Fix (F): *The Fifteen-Minute Fix*

The Action: Set a *Micro-Boundary*. If your schedule is out of alignment, find one fifteen-minute block in your day that is *sacred*. Whether it's having your coffee in silence or taking a walk around the block, you reclaim that small piece of territory.

The Replacement (R): *The Script Change*

The Action: Initiate a *New Terms* Conversation. You sit down with that person (or yourself) and say: "I've realized that the way we've been doing this isn't sustainable for me anymore. Moving forward, I can still help with [X], but I can no longer do [Y]."

The Gut Job (G): *The Stop-Work Order*

The Action: Go *Cold Turkey* on the Energy Drain. If it's a toxic habit or a mindset, you stop *managing* it and you cut it off. Block the number, delete the app, or walk away. You stop pouring your good energy into bad wood.

Clearing the Air: Atmospheric Actions

The Fix-Up: *The Sensory Reset*

The Action: Perform a *Surface Sweep*. Pick the one area where you spend the most time. Clear it completely. Put on a playlist that makes you feel the way you want to feel. You reset the *air quality* of your immediate space.

The Replacement (R): *The Input Filter*

The Action: Swap one *Drain* for one *Fill*. If you spend your first 20 minutes scrolling news that makes you anxious, replace it for three days with a book, a walk, or prayer. You are retrofitting your ventilation system.

The Gut Job (G): *The Eviction Notice*

The Action: Declare a *Sanctuary Zone*. Identify the source of the toxicity and physically or digitally remove yourself from it. You have to stop the *leak* before you can finally breathe deep.

IV. Wait! The Door is Stuck (Locating the Resistance)

Alright, Sis. Put that coffee mug in the sink. The plan is set, the junk is hauled away, and the foundation is finally cured. It's a beautiful day out there, and I think it's time we stop talking about what could be and go see what is. Let's head over to your place. Grab your keys—it's time to start framing.

You've got your tools and your blueprint, but I noticed something when you tried to head into the house—you pulled on that handle, and the door didn't budge. You rattled it, you shouldered it, and now you're looking at me like, "See? This is why I can't get anything done."

I hear you. It's frustrating when you finally find the "want-to," but the "how-to" feels jammed. In a renovation, a stuck door usually isn't because the door is "bad." It's usually because the house has shifted, the frame is out of place, or there's rust in the hinge that you can't even see. When you feel stuck in your life, it's rarely a lack of willpower. Usually, it's because your "internal handbrake" is pulled up tight. You're hitting the gas, but your tires are squealing because a part of you is terrified to move.

V. Locating the Block

To unjam the door, we have to find out where it's catching. Most of the time, the resistance comes down to one of three hidden fears:

- **Fear of Unknown Success (The Identity Crisis):** Success means things change. If you actually build this new life, you might not recognize the woman in the mirror. You're staying stuck because, yes, the *Old House* is uncomfortable, but at least you know where the light switches are.

- **Fear of Imperfection (The Analysis Paralysis):** This is procrastination wearing a ballgown. You tell yourself you're "researching" or "waiting for the right time," but really, you're just terrified of making a mistake. You're so worried about the "paint color" being wrong when you haven't even put up the walls.

- **Fear of Emotional Vulnerability:** This is when you've linked your self-worth to the outcome. You feel like if the renovation fails, you are a failure. To protect your heart, you just don't start.

Renovation Work Orders: Unjamming Techniques

The 5-Minute Rule: When the door feels too heavy to move, stop trying to open it all the way. Just crack it open for five minutes. Do the smallest possible version of the task. Action is the only thing that thins out fear. Once the door moves an inch, the rest of the opening gets easier.

The Post-it Vision: Because that *mind monster* loves to show up when you're tired, you need a visual reminder. Write your "next" on a Post-it note and stick it on the bathroom mirror. It shouldn't say "Fix my whole life." It should say: "I deserve a house that feels like peace."

The Vocal Contract: Say it out loud! There is power in your voice. Just hearing yourself say what you will do makes it even more real. Speak it out loud as many times as you need to until you believe it.

Speak It Out Loud:

I am unjamming this door. I am moving past [insert fear] and taking this ground today.

The door isn't locked, Sis—it's just tight. Give it one more pull. Now that the door is unjammed and you've declared war in the room, the path is clear. But opening the door is just the beginning. On the other side of that door is the old material that's been holding you back—the rotted wood, the outdated fixtures, and the walls that are blocking your view of the sun.

The door is open. Now, let's make sure we don't trip over the threshold as we head into the demo.

5

It's Demolition Time

Tearing Down to Build Up

Alright, Sis, put your goggles on and grab your heavy-duty gloves, because we're about to get our hands dirty. I've got mine on, too—I'm not just watching you swing that hammer; I'm holding the flashlight.

You drank your coffee, we've come to your house, we've unjammed the door, and now we're standing in the room that needs the most work. You see those old, stained carpets and those walls and cabinets that are closing you in? It's time for them to go.

In a real renovation, you can't install beautiful new cabinets if the old, water-damaged ones are still hanging on the wall. You can't put down hardwood over a floor that's rotted through. Most people try to renovate their lives by just adding new things—new habits, new friends, new goals. But if you keep adding new on top of rotted, you're just hiding the problem, not fixing it. A true transformation requires a teardown. We have to remove the structures that are no longer safe to lean on.

I. The Load-Bearing Lies

In a house, a load-bearing wall holds up the roof. In your life, you have *Load-Bearing Lies*—beliefs you've leaned on for so long that you think you'll collapse without them. Maybe it's the lie that you're only worthy when you're taking care of everyone else, or that if you showed your true self, you'd be rejected. We aren't just painting these walls; we are taking a sledgehammer to them. When you tear down a lie, it feels scary because for a moment, the roof feels unsupported. But remember: your Pillars—those core values we identified—are what actually hold you up. These lies were just temporary supports that are now in the way of your view.

Identifying the Load-Bearing Lies (The Inspection) Before we start swinging, we have to know what we're hitting. A *load-bearing lie* is sneaky—it disguises itself as *responsibility*, *safety*, or *just the way things are*. To find them, you have to look for the places where you feel the most trapped or heavy.

Here is your Inspection Checklist to find the lies holding up your old roof:

The "If I Don't" Test: Finish this sentence: "If I don't do [X], then [Y] will happen."

Example: "If I don't say yes to every request, then people will realize I'm selfish and leave me."

The Lie: Your worth is tied to your usefulness.

The "Always/Never" Scan: Listen to your internal dialogue. Wherever you hear the words *Always* or *Never*, there is usually a lie nearby.

Example: "I'll always be the one who gets left," or "I never get it right the first time."

The Lie: Your past failures are a permanent blueprint for your future.

The Exhaustion Audit: Look at the things that leave you feeling bone-tired and resentful. Usually, we do these things because we think we have to for the structure to stay up.

Example: Staying in a toxic friendship because "I'm the only one they can talk to."

The Lie: You are responsible for other people's emotional construction.

II. The Messy Middle: Salvage vs. Scrap

Here is the part no one tells you: once you start the demolition, your life is going to look like a wrecking zone. When you stop people-pleasing, people are going to get upset. When you quit a toxic habit, you're going to feel the dust of discomfort settling in your lungs. You're going to look around at the rubble and think, "I should have just left it alone." Don't you dare glue that drywall back up! No ma'am, don't even think about it! Leave it alone, back away and breathe. The mess is proof of progress.

As you sort through the debris, you have to be a master curator. You have to decide what is *scrap* and what is *salvage*. The *Scrap* is the dumpster material—the regret over years wasted, the lead-paint expectations of other people, and the identity of being a *victim*. Toss it all.

But the *Salvage* is your reclaimed wood. This is the wisdom you gained from the leaks, the strength you found when the house shook, and the hard-won discernment that knows exactly what rot smells like. We're going to sand those lessons down and make them centerpieces in your new home. Your past is not a weight; it is a warehouse of materials for your future.

III. Hauling the Junk and Pouring the Foundation

Once the walls are down, you have to get the debris off the property. When you start putting piles of junk on the curb, the neighbors—and even your own inner critic—are going to notice. They might try to talk you into keeping the trash because *that's the you they liked.* But this is your house and you are the only one who has a say here. You're going to have to be ruthless—that material is no longer up to code for where you're headed.

With the site finally clear, you can look down and see the Foundation. This is the underground work that no one sees but everyone relies on. We're pouring a new slab of Integrity (doing what you said you'd do for yourself), Stability (your daily routines), and Waterproofing (your boundaries). This is the expensive, quiet work that ensures the new house won't shift when the next storms come.

IV. Site Prep: Getting Ready for the Foundation

Now that we've identified the *Load-Bearing Lies* and started the demolition, we can't just leave a pile of debris and hope for the best. We have to prepare the ground. A life renovation isn't a weekend sprint; it's a process of clearing out the old to make room for the new. To keep from getting overwhelmed by the dust of your past, we use these three site-prep moves.

But before we pick up the tools, we need a set of *Site Rules*. These are the three Golden Rules of construction that we are going to use in every single phase of this build:

1. **The Domino Move:** Find your *One Thing.* Identify one single, 30-day habit—like waking up 30 minutes earlier

or drinking your water—that creates the space you need to work. When you're in the middle of a *Gut Job*, you need one thing that stays consistent. Focus on that one habit until it's your anchor.

2. **Build the Fence, Not the Willpower:** Stop relying on your feelings to get through the demolition phase—your feelings are valid, but they shift like the wind. Design your environment so you don't have to feel like doing the work. If you want peace, build a *fence* by putting the phone in another room at 9:00 PM. Don't fight your willpower; just change the layout so the junk can't get back in.

3. **Keep the Scoreboard:** In a renovation, the progress is often hidden behind the dust. You need a *Victory Log*. Every night, write down one small win—a lie you didn't believe, a boundary you stood by, or just the fact that you showed up for yourself today.

Renovation Work Order: The Demo List

Mark the Walls: Take a piece of paper and draw a line down the middle. On the left, write down three things you are terrified would happen if you stopped *performing* or *pleasing*. On the right, write down the truth (The Pillar) that actually supports you.

The Safety Check: Ask yourself: "Is this belief protecting me, or is it just keeping me small?" If it's keeping you small, it's not a support beam; it's a cage.

Swing the Hammer: Pick the smallest lie first. This week, purposefully do the opposite of what the lie tells you. If the lie says, "You have to finish everyone's work or the office will collapse," leave at 5:00 PM. Watch the roof stay up.

The Guest List Audit: Identify one person who keeps trying to put junk back onto your cleared site. Give them a polite, firm *Return to Sender* by not engaging in their drama today.

Speak It Out Loud:

I am tearing down the lies I've learned to lean on. My worth is not a weight I have to carry; it is a gift I already possess. I am safe without these walls of lies. The site is cleared and the junk is gone. I am not afraid of the dust because I am excited for the view. I am preparing this ground for a foundation that is set to last.

6

PUTTING UP THE FRAMING

DEFINING THE NEW ROOMS

Look at this foundation, Sis! It looks even bigger now that we're standing on it. Now comes the part where we start to see the shape of things. We're moving from *tearing down* to *putting up*. But here is the secret to a good frame: a room is only as good as the walls that define it. I want you to look at this space—we aren't just building walls; we're defining your life.

If you don't frame your rooms correctly, your *Office* starts bleeding into your *Living Room*, and your *Guest Room*—the space you give to others—starts taking over your *Master Suite*, which is your private, internal peace. Framing is the art of saying: "This is what happens here, and this is what does not happen here."

I. Hard Studs and Soft Spaces

In framing, you have *hard studs* and *soft spaces*. The *studs* are your non-negotiable boundaries. These are the things that give your life its shape. If your pillar is *Integrity*, then a hard boundary is deciding that you will no longer lie to protect someone else's comfort. These walls don't move; they provide the strength for the roof to sit on.

The *soft spaces* are your doors. You have to decide who gets a key and who has to knock. If you leave your life without doors, you're just a public park, and everyone will walk through your flowerbeds. You are in charge of the guest list.

II. Squaring the Corners

A critical part of this phase is *squaring the corners*. If a frame isn't square, the doors won't swing right and the floors will eventually creak. Squaring your life means making sure your daily actions are perfectly aligned with your stated values. If you say you value *Presence*, but your *Office* takes up 90% of your calendar, your house is out of square. We measure the corners by looking at our time and our energy—they don't lie.

III. The Open Concept Life

When we talk about the *layout* of your new life, we are aiming for an open concept. Now, don't get nervous—this doesn't mean you have no privacy or that everyone gets to see your business. It means you have transparency and accountability.

In your old house, you had tiny, dark closets where you stuffed your shame, your secrets, and the parts of yourself you thought were *unmarketable*. But when you have those closed-off, unventilated spaces, that's exactly where the mold of old habits starts to grow. You can't heal what you're hiding.

Building an open concept life means we are tearing down the *shame walls*. We are building a life where the light of your truth can reach every single corner. Maintenance looks a little different in an open concept house where you can't just take the junk and throw it behind a closed door. When you are transparent with yourself—and with the few *Key-Holders* which we'll talk about later—you take away the power of the rot. There's a freedom that comes when you no longer have to remember which lie you told in which room. In this house, the truth is the foundation, and the light is the decor.

IV. Setting the Layout: Applying Your Site Rules

Now that the ground is level, we don't rush into buying curtains. We have to set the layout for a build that lasts. Remember those *Site Rules* we established during demolition? Here is how we use them to get these walls up:

1. **The Domino Move:** As we frame these rooms, identify the one habit that makes the rest of the house stand tall. If you get your *Morning Peace* stud straight, the *Work Room* walls will be much easier to nail into place.

2. **Build the Fence, Not the Willpower:** Now that we are defining rooms, the *Fence* is even more important. You don't need willpower to keep people out of your *Inner Sanctum* if you've built a door and locked it. Design the layout so you don't have to fight yourself.

3. **Keep the Scoreboard:** We aren't just tracking *junk hauled* anymore; we're tracking *studs placed*. Every night in your *Victory Log*, celebrate a moment where you stood your ground or defined a boundary.

Renovation Work Order: The Framing Session

Define Your Rooms: Identify one area where the walls have been too thin—where people walk all over you—and decide exactly where the new line goes.

Install the Door: Pick one person who has "all-access" and require them to "knock" (ask) before entering your private emotional space.

The Site Visit: Identify one *Key-Holder* from your inner circle. Share one specific boundary you're working on and ask: "I'm trying to keep this corner square. Can you check in on me next week?"

The Square Check: Measure your last 48 hours against your pillars. If your time doesn't align with your values, you're *out of square*. Adjust tomorrow's schedule to fix the lean.

Speak It Out Loud:

I am defining my space. I decide what stays out and what stays in. My life is balanced, my corners are square. I invite the light into every room I build. I am strong enough to be seen, and I am wise enough to let the right people hold me to my own standard. My life is an open book to the ones I trust, and a solid wall to the ones I don't.

V. The Footing Inspection: Challenging Inner Assumptions

Let's challenge some inner assumptions. I know we talked about this a little bit in Chapter 5, but I want to take it a bit deeper. These are the kind you don't speak out loud because—*gasp*—some of them may be shameful, but they dictate how you operate.

You run yourself ragged because you truly believe things will fall apart if you're not there to anticipate and fix. You are constantly inwardly criticizing your coworkers, spouse, children, and self because you truly don't believe that you measure up and somehow everyone else's misgivings reflect on you.

What you don't realize is that others are reading these inward convictions loud and clear, whether you say them or not. Your actions, your tone, your fears, and your questions are all betraying your truth. So how do we fix this?

Shed light to your truth. The whole truth—even the dastardly, ugly parts. Then confront, examine, and explore those assumptions. What would happen if you called in sick? What if your kid was the loud, obnoxious one at the party? What if your husband picked out his own clothes and they—*gasp*—didn't perfectly match your own?

The sun would still shine. The sky would still be there. People would laugh and still consider your child well-mannered on the whole, and you may actually be a happier couple, even if the colors clashed.

VI. The Source vs. The Solution

Oftentimes we get stuck on the origins of these misgivings. We want to know exactly which storm caused the crack or which previous tenant left the mess. While this can produce useful insight, the real question is: How do you choose to move forward?

Just because you were criticized or emotionally neglected as a child—or whatever your specific case may be—doesn't mean that you are unworthy of love and appreciation. It most certainly doesn't mean that you are doomed to repeat this pattern going forward.

Cycle breakers are simply the people who choose to make a different choice.

Is that you?

VII. Moving from Tongue to Deed

Besides examining, we now have a choice to make: either keep operating as is, even when the truth has been revealed, or start making some different choices to relinquish control. Naturally, you're going to say "relinquish control," but it's much easier said than done.

To actually move forward in deed and not just in tongue, we have to stop talking about "letting go" and start practicing the mechanics of it.

The Mechanics of Relinquishment

- **The "Wait and See" Strategy:** Set a timer for 15 minutes before jumping in to fix a situation. Let it resolve without you.

- **The "Clash" Test:** Intentionally allow something small to be imperfect. Let the colors clash.

- **Delegation Without Editing:** Give a task away and do not fix it when it's done. If it functions, it's a success.

- **The Silence Audit:** Ask yourself: *"Is this my house to build, or theirs?"* If it's theirs, be a neighbor, not the foreman.

The Contractor's Challenge: The Controlled Collapse

Choose **one** "minor" structure to let fail this week:

- **The Mismatched Day:** Let a family member clash outfits with you in public. Do not fix it.

- **The Silence Strike:** Wait 30 minutes before "fixing" a ball someone else dropped.

- **The Unvetted Project:** Delegate a task and accept the result exactly as it is returned to you.

Every time you catch yourself leaning back into that lie, take a breath, say your mantra, and choose differently.

Speak It Out Loud:

My foundation is firm. This is their room to build, not mine to fix.

Renovation Work Order: The Assumption Audit

- **Identify the "Structural Ghost":** Write down one specific situation this week where you felt "run ragged." What was the unspoken assumption dictating your panic?

- **The Flashlight Test:** Write down one thing you've been hiding—even from yourself—and bring it into the light of your journal. Name it to lose its power. Is that assumption a fact or a fear? Write the *fact* next to it to strip the fear of its authority.

- **The "Reflection" Purge:** Identify one person whose "misgivings" you have been carrying as your own. Mentally hand that baggage back to them.

Speak It Out Loud:

I am done with the dark. I invite the light into every room I build. I am strong enough to be seen, and I am wise enough to let the right people hold me to my own standard.

7

THE ROUGH-IN

PLUMBING, WIRING, AND CLIMATE CONTROL

We've got the rooms framed out! It's looking like a real house now. But stand still for a second. We can see the rooms, but we can't feel the flow yet. While the walls are still open, we have to get behind the drywall to the plumbing and the wiring. If we put up the walls now, we'll just be standing in a pretty shed. We need this house to actually work for you!

The *Rough-In* phase is about the systems that run behind the scenes. It's the stuff no one else sees, but it's the difference between a life that's functional and a life that's exhausting.

I. The Plumbing: Emotional Drainage

A house needs a way to bring in fresh water and a way to carry waste away. What are you pouring into your spirit? Are you hooked up to sources of life like silence, joy, and truth? And just as importantly, how are you processing your waste—your anger, your grief, and your stress? If you don't have a system for drainage, like journaling or moving your body, that emotional waste stays in the house and starts to smell.

We've talked about the guests you allow in, but we also have to be careful of how we show up in our own space. I don't know about you, but a stuffy, cluttered room just automatically makes me feel uptight and irritated. Taking a minute to declutter and open up the windows makes a world of difference. The same is true with your emotions—when is the last time you took time to declutter your spirit?

We hold on to so much stuff without even realizing it. It comes up in our dreams, our musings, or in the shower when we're thinking about nothing. At some point, like we said about the onion, you just have to make a choice. If something keeps creeping up and making you feel *some type of way*—release it! Choose to release it. Say it out loud and keep saying it until it becomes real for you:

I choose to release this feeling. I choose to release this person. I choose to release this situation. I may not have handled it the best, or they may not have handled me the best, but I choose to learn from it, release the hurt, pain, and bitterness of it, and move forward with my life.

I know we've mentioned it a couple of times now, but it bears mentioning again—be mindful of what you allow into your space! You are taking the time to find healthy outlets for your *Emotional Drainage*; do not allow others to dump their emotional garbage on you. If that means that you need to nicely cut a conversation short, or heck, just not answer the phone—do it for you, boo boo!

If someone has already dumped on you, release it! That is their dirt to deal with. Love them, pray for them, wish them well, but their mess is not yours to pick up. You aren't a landfill; you're a sanctuary.

To keep the lines clear, you need a *Movement Flush*. Emotions are physical, Sis—that's why they show up in our body as illnesses, aches, and pains. Sometimes you can't think your way out of a clog; you have to move it. A 10-minute walk or stretching helps your body process the stress that's sitting in your pipes. And at the end of the day, use the *Brain Dump Valve*: write down every worry—yours and the stuff people tried to hand you—and get it out of the house.

You don't need that toxicity bubbling over into the rest of your life and impacting the way you operate. People don't want to be around you because you're always miserable and angry—no Sis, that is not cute! We all know those type of people and they all make us want to run away and hide! You were called to be a woman of beauty and substance inside and out, so release it and let it go so that you can be everything that you were destined to be.

II. The Wiring: Your Power Grid

Next, we check the wiring—your nervous system. This is your *Power Grid*. You can't run a modern home on a 1950s fuse box. It's no wonder you're blowing breakers every Tuesday—you're plugging in too many demands with not enough recharge time.

You need to know what *trips your breaker*. What are your triggers? What sends you into a total blackout? You have to wire in your rest. Rest isn't a luxury you get when the work is finished; it's the power source that allows the work to happen.

Now, listen to me: we often think of a trigger as that one big thing that makes us snap. But that's not usually how it works. That snap happens when too much stuff has piled up and accumulated without being cleared away.

- **The Jenga Tower:** It starts out whole and strong, but as the bricks of rest and peace are pulled out one by one, the whole thing starts to wobble.

- **The Cracking Ice:** It's not just that last step that caused the break; it's the totality of the weight that's been stacked on top of it for weeks. It's the *death by a thousand cuts*, or in this case, death by a thousand *yeses* when you should have said *no*.

I really want the best for you, so please, please, please pay attention to your body and begin to say no and rest when you know your battery is running low. Don't get to empty and now you're stuck on the side of the road calling for help before you take a minute to recharge.

When you're at 20% battery, go into low-power mode. Shut down the non-essential apps—say no to the extra meetings—and save that last bit of juice for you. I am not having any *Black Screens of Death* on my watch!

Now Sis, I know you, because I do it, too—let's be honest. Rest is not the 15 minutes you spend watching TV while folding laundry or sitting down while chopping veggies for your weekly meal prep. It's not the 30 minutes in a massage chair while you're still sending emails and ordering your groceries. No ma'am!

True rest is that *do nothing but lay in this bed until you're tired of laying in it* kind of rest. The kind where your shoulders finally drop and gives you a good belly laugh. You cannot give from an empty well and you are not fully recharging if you're working while resting—it's kind of like when you're using your phone while its plugged in. Yes, it will recharge, but it takes twice as long and isn't as effective—depending on the charging type, you may still be burning more battery even though its plugged in, and the last thing I want to see you do is burn out. No *Black Screens of Death* are happening on my watch ma'am. So go for a drive out in the country with the windows down, grab an ice cream, take a hike or a walk in the park. Do something that is going to truly allow you to breathe, and do it regularly. Everything else can wait until you return, but if you allow yourself to rest, you'll actually be able to do more efficiently.

III. The HVAC: Setting the Climate

Finally, we look at the *HVAC*, which sets your internal climate. Most people act like thermometers; they just reflect the temperature of the room they walk into. If the world is chaotic, they get chaotic.

But you are the thermostat. You have the power to set the internal climate of your soul. No matter how cold or hot the situation gets outside, your internal system can be calibrated to keep you at a steady, unwavering peace.

There's this saying, *I match energy, so how are "we" gonna act today*—that is one of the most ridiculous things I have ever heard. No ma'am, I am a queen. I set the tone and regardless of how you choose to treat me, I will not be bullied, begged, or duped off of my throne and the people and situations around me adjust to me, not the other way around.

Now I know this is easier said than done, but look, we're going to do our best to straighten our crown and keep it pushing. As you continue to do the work of regulating your emotions and your nervous system, this gets so much easier. As women, we have to learn to embrace being and breathing.

IV. Applying Your Site Rules

1. **The Domino Move:** Your *One Thing* is *System Maintenance*. If you keep your drainage clear, every other room in the house stays fresh. Focus on the habit of daily release.

2. **Build the Fence, Not the Willpower:** Instead of exhausting yourself trying to be strong, we are doing the *What Did You Do For Yourself?* Challenge. We're building a fence made of self-investment. Design your day so that your fence is one intentional act of kindness toward yourself.

3. **Keep the Scoreboard:** Your *Victory Log* for this chapter is about self-regulation. Did you take a *Bumper Breath*? Did you complete your daily challenge? Record those wins!

Renovation Work Order: The Systems Check

Clear the Clog: Identify one emotional drain that is backed up—a conversation you're avoiding or a resentment you've been nursing. Open the valve and clear it today through prayer, journaling, or a direct conversation.

Map Your Breaker Box: Identify the biggest energy drain of your week. Label it. Now, decide today how you will limit the power you send to that specific drain so you stop blowing your circuits.

Calibrate the Thermostat: Before you walk into your next challenging room (a meeting, a difficult house, a stressful appointment), stop. Take three deep breaths and manually set your internal thermostat to *Peace*. Do not let the room change you; you change the room.

True Plug-In: Schedule one hour this week for *unproductive rest*. No phone, no chores, no mental to-do lists. Just recharge.

Flush the System: Tonight, do a 5-minute *Brain Dump*. Write down any dirt that isn't yours and visualize yourself handing it back to its owner before you close the notebook.

The Jenga Check: Look at your week. Which brick of rest or hobbies have you pulled out lately? Put it back in today.

Speak It Out Loud:

My house is a sanctuary, not a landfill. I am hooked up to life-giving sources, and I have a system to drain the stress. I am responsible for my peace, so I release what isn't mine and I keep my lines clear. I am not the neighborhood garbage man; I am the thermostat of my own soul. My internal systems are clear and strong, and I will not be blown off-course by the weather outside. Today, I choose to invest in myself because I am worth the maintenance.

8

Insulation and Drywall

Protecting the Progress

We've got the framing up, and the plumbing and wiring are running smooth. Now, it's time for the silent hero of the home: *Insulation.* You never see insulation, but you definitely feel it when it's missing. Its only job is to keep the outside from dictating the inside. This is where the house stops being just a structure and starts becoming a place of comfort and safety.

Now, I know what you're thinking: "Sis, didn't we just talk about self-care and drainage in the last chapter?" Yes, we did. But there is a big difference between *Plumbing* and *Insulation.* *Plumbing* is how you handle the mess once it's already inside the house. *Insulation* is what keeps the cold of the world from seeping through the cracks to begin with. If you don't insulate your life, you'll spend all your energy—and all your heating bill—trying to maintain your peace while the world is constantly sucking it out of you.

I. The Thermal Barrier of Consistency

In construction, insulation is measured by its *R-value*. All that means is how well a material resists the transfer of heat. The higher the *R-value*, the better it protects your internal climate. In your life, we increase our *R-value* with *Consistent Habits*. Think of it like this: Chapter 7 was about the tools you use when things get heavy, but Chapter 8 is about the rhythms that keep you from feeling the weight to begin with.

When you have a solid routine of quiet time, reflection, and physical rest, you are adding a thick layer of resistance to your soul. Without it, every little draft makes your internal temperature drop. You end up cranking up your internal heater—your stress response—just to stay at your baseline. That is why you're exhausted! You aren't just living your life; you're fighting the elements because your walls are thin and drafty.

Remember, if the *Blueprint* we drew in Chapter 4 was shaky, the house is even harder to keep warm. A well-designed life keeps the heat in without you having to fight for it. This is not the cabin in *Little House on the Prairie*, ma'am; this is your luxury mansion—we need your home to be 100% sealed and leak-free.

II. Noise Insulation: Muffling the Critics

Have you ever stayed in a hotel where the walls were paper-thin? You could hear the TV next door and every conversation in the hallway. Even if you were in a nice room, you couldn't actually relax because the outside noise was constant. A lot of us are living our lives with paper-thin walls. We are too *acoustically accessible*. We hear every opinion, every "I wouldn't do it that way," and every "Did you hear what she did?" It leaves us either distracted with other people's issues or questioning our own capability. Either way, we are now ineffective, tired, and worn out. It is madness and it needs to stop!

Noise Insulation is the practice of muffling the voices that don't belong in your room. When you are well-insulated, people may be talking, but they sound like they're miles away. You can see their lips moving, but you can't hear the words. This isn't about being stuck up; it's about being *soundproof*. You have to muffle the crowd so you can hear your own heart without the sound system feedback.

III. Fire Protection: Support Without the Scorch

In a real build, they use *fire-rated drywall* and *fire-caulk* in the gaps to prevent a fire in one area from spreading to the rest of the house. Sis, you have to install some *Fire Protection* in your life. We all have people whose lives are constantly on fire. You're probably thinking of one person like that right now. If you aren't careful, their fire will jump the gap and start burning down your new *Kitchen*—and baby, you worked hard for that beautiful new *Kitchen*, so we are not having that!

Now I know you feel torn because you want to be a good friend, but there is a huge difference between holding a flashlight for someone and stepping into the fire with them. So how do you support them without getting scorched yourself in the process? I'm so glad you asked.

First, you have to be a listener, not a fixer. When someone is in a blaze of drama, they often want you to help them move the furniture while the house is still burning. Don't do it. You can say, "I hear how hard this is," without offering to make the phone calls, pay the bills, or confront the person they're fighting with.

You also have to check the wind direction. Before you engage, ask yourself if this person is looking for a solution, or if they are just looking for a new place for the fire to spread. If they've had the same fire every week for three years, they aren't looking for an extinguisher; they're looking for an audience. You can even ask them, "Hey, do you need a listening ear, or do you need me to do something?" This may even help them realize what they're doing and stop.

Finally, remember the power of *hopeful distance*. Sometimes the most supportive thing you can do is stay on your own property and send good vibes their way. You aren't being mean; you're being responsible for the structure that is yours to manage. *Fire Protection* is the ability to say: "I love you and I'm concerned about you, but I'm not letting that fire into my house."

IV. Closing the Walls: The Drywall

Then comes the *Drywall*. This is the skin of the room. It covers the messy wires and the silver pipes. In your life, the *Drywall* is your *Public Presentation*. For a long time, you might have lived with your *wires exposed*—letting everyone see your trauma, your process, and your mess before it was healed. And while I totally understand why you did it, it also exposed you—and others—to some risk.

See, in a build, when the electrician is messing with the wiring, the power is usually turned off to decrease the risk of a shock. Raw wires—your raw emotions—can shock the heck out of you and the people around you. It can cause you to show a side of you that you may not always be proud of, and that costs you something. Some people have been shocked by our raw emotions and have shied away from us, costing us relationships, opportunities, and our reputation.

Hanging the *Drywall* means you've reached a level of maturity where you choose what to show the world. It's not about being fake; it's about being finished. You only invite your *Faithful Few* to help you with moving day, but you invite others to your housewarming once the curtains are hung and the paint has dried. Not everyone needs to be a part of your private journey. And for goodness sake, please do not post all of that on social media! We don't do it for the 'gram—we do it because we want to be whole. Protect what you have worked so hard to build! Everyone cannot carry your emotions, and not everyone should be invited to that work.

What Does "Healing in Private" Actually Mean?

I want to be very clear here: closing the walls is not about concealing your pain; it's about *containing* it. There is a massive difference. *Concealing* is when you pretend the exposed wires aren't there, which eventually leads to a fire. *Containing* is when you admit the wiring is dangerous and you bring in a professional to help you fix it while the room is closed to the public.

When we talk about *healing in private*, we mean three specific things:

- **Managing the Surge:** When you are raw, your emotions

are like live wires. If you touch them, you get shocked. If someone else touches them, they get shocked. Healing in private means you stop letting the world touch your raw spots before you've had a chance to put the protective coating back on your nerves. It means you take your heavy grief, your burning anger, or your deep confusion to a safe place—a counselor, a trusted mentor, or your journal—rather than live-streaming your process to people who aren't equipped to help you fix the problem.

- **Protecting the Cure Time:** In a house, when you apply mud to the drywall seams, it has to dry. If you try to sand it or paint it while it's still wet, you'll ruin the finish. Your healing has a *cure time*, too. When you share your process too early with the wrong people, their opinions, their "I told you so's," or even their well-meaning advice can act like a draft that cracks your wet plaster. Healing in private means you give your new perspective time to *set* and become solid before you subject it to the elements.

- **Choosing Your Job Site Crew:** Just because the walls are up doesn't mean you are in the house alone. It just means you've stopped letting the nosey neighbors and busybodies through the construction zone. Healing in private means you invite the *Electrician* (the professional who can actually help) and the *Faithful Few* (the friends who don't mind the dust) into the room with you. You are still doing the work; you're just doing it behind a door that has a lock on it.

The Voltage Test: How to Know You're Ready

In a real renovation, an electrician uses a voltage tester to see if a wire is hot before they seal it away. You can do the same thing with your heart. You know you're *healed enough* to close the walls when you pass these three tests:

1. **The Trigger Test (The Shock Factor):** When you think about that situation, that person, or that trauma, do you still get a physical shock to your system? If mentioning it makes your heart race, your palms sweat, or your voice shake with a power surge of anger or grief, the wire is still raw. You're ready for the *Drywall* when it becomes a part of your story instead of a live current that knocks you off your feet.

2. **The Mud and Tape Test (The Smooth Finish):** Healing isn't just about stopping the pain; it's about smoothing the edges. When you first start working through something, the seams of your life are rough and jagged. You know you're ready to present that room to the world when you've sanded it down. This means you've

processed the why and the how, and you aren't looking for every person you meet to help you smooth it out. If you're still looking for validation from strangers to tell you you're okay, the mud is still wet.

3. **The Housewarming Test (The Intent)**: Ask yourself: "Am I sharing this to help someone else, or am I sharing this so someone will help me?" If you are still bleeding for an audience, or dumping your pain when you say it, you aren't ready to close the wall. But, if you can look at your process and say, "I want to show people this finished room so they know it's possible to build one too," then you are ready.

It's not about being perfect, Sis. You close the walls so you can finally live in the room, rather than just laboring in it. Growth often feels like *narrowing* because you're no longer spread thin across a construction site; you are focused within your walls. You aren't shrinking; you are contained, you are whole, and you are leak-free.

Renovation Work Order: The Sound & Safety Check

The Ear or Action Drill: The next time a friend on fire calls, ask the question: "Do you need an ear or an action?" If they just need an ear, set a personal time limit and exit the conversation when the fire starts to spread toward your property.

Consistency Check: Pick one small habit—silence, a short walk, or a specific morning routine—and do it at the same time every day this week. This is how you seal the drafts in your *Insulation.*

The Mud & Tape Phase: Look for a seam in your life where your private business is leaking into your public world. Maybe you've been too raw with a coworker or over-sharing on a group chat. Today, apply a layer of *joint compound*—decide that this specific topic is now officially behind the walls until it's fully healed and sanded smooth.

Muffle the Noise: Identify one noisy voice that makes you question your capabilities and mute the volume today. Notice the warmth that returns to your home when the draft is gone.

Speak It Out Loud:

My home is soundproof, insulated, and fire-rated. I am not a lifeboat; I am a lighthouse. I choose what to show the world, and I keep my private work private. My home is safe and I am whole. My walls are solid, my peace is insulated, my progress is protected, and I am no longer a drafty house. What happens inside these walls is sacred, and I am the one who sets the temperature.

9

WINDOWS AND DOORS

THE ENVELOPE

The walls are up, and the drywall is smooth, but a house without windows is a bunker, and a house without doors is a prison. In construction, we call the windows and doors the *Envelope*. They are the intentional openings that allow for light, air, and access. Up until now, we've been focused on the bones and the skin of the house, but now we have to talk about your *Outlook* and your *Threshold*.

I. Acknowledging the *New House* Nerves

Before we pick up the drill, let's be real: this part is going to feel uncomfortable. If you have spent your whole life with a beaded curtain instead of a front door, you've been letting in every draft and critic we tried to block out in the last chapter. Installing a deadbolt is going to feel aggressive. Now if you're the kind of person who is quick to block someone, you may need to put the drill down, pause and be a little more strategic—we're going for boundaries in balance.

You also need to be prepared: others may react negatively to you finally putting your foot down. People who are used to having free reign of your construction site aren't going to like it when they see a locked door. They might get angry, they might try to guilt-trip you, or they might sit on your porch knocking for hours hoping you'll reconsider. Don't! If they act out, give them a big smile, wish them well, and still close and lock that door. Then, walk back into your peaceful living room, turn on your favorite show, grab a piece of cake and put your feet up while you eat it. Celebrate yourself for establishing a boundary! Boundary-setting is a muscle; it feels weak at first, but eventually, people will get used to the new strength of your door. If they choose not to respect it, well, that just shows more of who they are. It is not your problem to adjust back to their dysfunction.

II. The Window Audit: Cleaning Your Perspective

Windows determine two things: how much light gets in and what you see when you look out. Remember, if your foundation is level and your framing is square, your windows won't crack when the pressure of life pushes against them. When your internal integrity is solid, your perspective stays clear; you aren't seeing the world through the cracks of your own unresolved stuff. If your windows are dirty, the whole world looks like a threat. To change your outlook, you have to realize the glass is dirty in the first place. Use these audit questions to see if your *Windows* are helping you or hindering you:

- **The Mirror Question:** Am I seeing this situation as it actually is, or am I seeing it through the fog of a past hurt?

- **The Warp Question:** Is this thought a *PROBABILITY* or just a *POSSIBILITY*? (It's possible everyone is judging you; it's probable they are just busy).

- **The Lighting Question:** If I were giving this same advice to a woman I loved, would it sound this harsh? If not, why am I letting that dark perspective live in my house?

- **The Horizon Question:** Am I staring at the dirt on the windowsill (the small daily stresses) or am I looking out at the horizon (the big picture)?

- **The Devil's Advocate:** Are there other perspectives or considerations I haven't considered yet? Is there a version of this story where I am safe and favored?

III. The Boundary Tool Kit: Scripts for the Peep Hole

If you struggle with boundaries, your biggest fear is the confrontation. These tools are designed to protect your space jedi-mind-trick style without you having to throw a single punch.

1. The Porch Light (The Signal) In the old days, if the porch light was off, it meant don't knock. You need a digital and emotional *Porch Light*. This means using *Do Not Disturb* modes or simply not responding to non-emergencies immediately. It signals to others—and reminds yourself—that you are not "on call" for the world. A simple, no or not now is all that is needed.

The Script: *I'm currently focusing on some housework (personal time/projects) and will be checking messages at 4:00 PM. If this is an emergency, please call 911. Otherwise, I'll get back to you soon!*

Why it works: It trains people to wait. It puts the *Porch Light* on for you so you don't have to explain why you didn't answer. It establishes that you are home but not available.

2. The Intercom System (The Buffer) Before you let someone into your mental space, use an *Intercom*. This looks like saying, "I can't talk right now, but you can text me what you need." It puts a layer of technology or time between their "emergency" and your peace. It allows you to process their request without the pressure of their presence.

The Script: *That sounds like a lot to handle. Let me sit with my schedule and see if I have the square footage (or bandwidth or capacity) for that right now. I'll let you know by tomorrow.*

Why it works: You aren't saying no yet; you're just stepping back from the door. It gives you the space to decide if you actually want to do it without the heat of their presence pressuring you.

3. The Property Line (Clear Signage) Sometimes people cross boundaries because they don't know where the line is. You need clear signage. This looks like the phrase: *I'm not open to feedback on this decision right now.* You aren't being mean; you're just marking the spot where your lawn begins and their sidewalk ends.

The Casual Pivot: *You know, I'm really trying to keep my head in a positive space today and talking about [Topic/Person] kind of drains my battery. Do you mind if we talk about something else?*

The Soft Boundary: *I've realized that I get a little stressed when we dive into [Topic/Person], and I'm really protective of my peace right now. Let's switch gears—tell me about [New Topic]!*

The Honest Direct: *I'm actually taking a break from [drama/gossip/work talk] today for my own sanity. Can we talk about something a little lighter?*

The Vibe Check: *Oof, I don't think I have the bandwidth in my brain to handle [Topic] today! Can we pivot? I'd much rather hear about your [Vacation/Project/Kids].*

Why it works: You aren't blaming them; you are taking responsibility for your home's climate. You're just pointing to the sign and asking them to respect the lawn.

4. The Exit Lighting (The Out): Every public building has an exit sign. You need one for your conversations. Have a pre-planned exit for when a boundary is being pushed. *It was great catching up, but I have to go now* is your emergency exit. You don't need a reason. You just need to follow the light to the door.

The Script: *I've hit my limit for the day and I need to protect my rest. Let's pick this up another time.*

Why it works: It's honest. You are the security guard of your own soul. If the room is at capacity and your energy is low, you have the right to clear it out.

Now when you say this, be ready to either grab your purse and walk out the door, give a goodbye and hang up the phone, or go into lockdown mode and just stop talking. For a person who is not good with respecting boundaries, or just not used to you establishing boundaries, this may seem to them to be an invitation to ask "why?" No is a complete sentence, and you've actually already given them more than that. Protect your peace at all costs and end the conversation as respectfully, yet definitively as possible.

Applying Your Site Rules

1. **The Domino Move: The 60-Minute Buffer.** When a request comes in, wait one hour before answering. Use that time to breathe and decide if you actually have the capacity.

2. **Build the Fence, Not the Willpower: Use the Scripts.** Write your *Intercom Script* on a sticky note and keep it near your phone. Don't try to wing it—let the signage do the work.

3. **Keep the Scoreboard: The Cake Moment.** Record every time you felt the guilt of a boundary but chose to celebrate yourself instead of giving in.

Renovation Work Order: Checking the Seals

Windex Your Vision: Apply a window audit question to one worry you have today. Write out three other possible (and positive) ways that situation could end.

The Shade Check: Pick one busybody who is always peeking into your business and simply pull the shades. You don't have to be mean; just stop providing the view. Practice the *Porch Light* signal—if you aren't available, don't answer the door or the text.

Check the Intercom: Use the *Square Footage* script at least once this week, even if it's for something small. Build the muscle before the heavy lifting starts.

Buffer the Busybody: Identify one nosey neighbor or busybody in your life who always tries to peek through the windows of your private business. Today, pull the shades—give them a *Porch Light* signal and don't engage in the gossip.

Speak it Out Loud:

I am the gatekeeper of my home and the protector of my view. I give myself permission to be uncomfortable while I learn to be secure. My "no" is a deadbolt, and my peace is a sanctuary. If others knock in anger, I will respond in love, but I will not open the door to chaos. My windows are clean, my doors are secure, and I will guard this home I worked so hard to build.

10

PAINT AND TRIM

THE BEAUTY OF THE BUILD

Look around, Sis. The dust has settled, the walls are smooth, the windows are sparkling, and the doors are locked tight. For the first time in a long time, the house is quiet. But it's a little plain, isn't it? It's solid, but it's missing your flavor. This is the phase where we stop talking about safety and structure and start talking about beauty. It's time to pick your colors.

I. Reclaiming Your Palette

For years, you might have been living in a house painted *People-Pleaser Beige* or *Survivor Gray*. You chose those colors because they were safe; they didn't attract too much attention, and they hid the dirt. It was the *Standard Floor Plan* the world expected of you. But you aren't a subdivision house anymore; you're a custom build.

Now that the rot is gone, you don't have to hide anymore. Reclaiming your *Paint and Trim* is about giving yourself permission to be vibrant again. You couldn't see these colors when the room was full of dust, but now that the air is clear, the light is hitting the walls differently. It's about shifting your question from "What makes me feel safe?" to "What makes me feel alive?"

Paint is the easiest thing to change, but it has the biggest impact on the vibe. In your life, your *Paint* is your attitude and expression. Are you choosing to coat your days in gratitude, or are you still stuck in the habit of expecting the worst? You get to dip your brush into a new bucket today. You can choose bold colors like *Courage*, *Playfulness*, or *Rest*. You aren't painting over the past; you're choosing the hue you want to live in now.

II. The Test Patch Approach

Now, we have all gone into a home improvement store and stared at the wall of paint swatches and suddenly felt overwhelmed. I need you to step back and breathe—paint is not permanent if you don't care for the color. We're going to take some baby steps. Pick a few trial-size tubs and try some things that you think may spark your joy. If you love it, go with it. If you hate it—no worries, paint over it!

They say it takes about a year for a person to truly move into a home, getting all the colors and textures just the way they like it. You have time to explore. You may pick a color and love it today—maybe you want to paint the whole house *Watch Out Now Red*—and then realize that color doesn't suit you for a Tuesday at the office. Perhaps in that space, you need *Dial It Back Black* (or *Charcoal*, really). That's okay! This is your life and your home, honey; all that matters is that you are happy in it. Choosing a calmer color for the *Office* isn't about hiding; it's about setting the climate so you can work without your wiring getting overheated.

III. The Finishing Touch: The Trim

In a house, the trim covers the gaps where the walls meet the floor. It's the finishing touch that makes everything look intentional. It is the ornate yet subtle features that make the room interesting and unique—the *Crown Jewel*, if you will. In your life, the *Trim* is the *Small Joys and Details*. It's the way you make your coffee in the morning, the music you play while you drive, and the hobbies you finally picked back up.

Without the *Trim*, the house feels raw and unfinished. With it, the house feels cared for, loved, and unique. Be careful, because the *Old You* might try to tell you that beauty is a waste of time. She might say, "We have too much work to do to worry about joy right now." But remember: you didn't do all that demolition just to live in a boring box. Your joy is not a luxury; it is the evidence of your hard-earned healing.

IV. The Joy-Permit: Finalizing the Finish Work

Before we wrap up this phase, we have to talk about the *Joy-Permit*. A lot of us fall into the *Punch List Fallacy*. In construction, there is always a list of tiny things—a loose screw here, a squeaky floorboard there—that still need fixing. You might think you can't enjoy the new paint while that one floorboard still squeaks, but perfection isn't a prerequisite for presence. Just because there's a tiny draft in the hallway doesn't mean you can't turn up the music and dance in the *Living Room*. Joy is not a reward for being done; it is the fuel that helps you finish the list.

As you start to explore these new colors, you'll be tempted to engage in *Vibe-Check Seeking*. When you pick a new hobby, a new style, or a new attitude, your instinct will be to call someone and ask, "Is this okay? Does this look like me?" But honey, if you have to ask someone else if you're allowed to like something, you're handing them the keys to your paint locker. For the next thirty days, I want you to treat your joy as a *Private Build*. You don't need a permit from anyone else to enjoy the colors you chose.

Finally, we have to do a *Cost-Per-Smile Analysis*. We often feel guilty spending time or money on things that aren't productive. But if a *Trim* detail—whether it's a fancy coffee or a new book—improves your internal climate, it is a *Maintenance Expense*, not a luxury. Keeping your spirit high is part of the property upkeep. It is much cheaper to buy the paint of joy now than it is to pay for another demolition of a burnout later.

Applying Your Site Rules

1. **The Domino Move: Trial-Size Joy.** Instead of just *doing* your morning routine, decorate it. Pick one small thing—a new candle or a specific playlist—that adds your flavor to the habit.

2. **Build the Fence, Not the Willpower: Protect the Wet Paint.** When you are trying out a new attitude or hobby, don't invite the critics over to see it yet. Let it dry before you ask for opinions. Keep the curtains closed while you're testing the swatches.

3. **Keep the Scoreboard: The Color Check.** At the end of the day, write down one thing that added color to your world. If it made you smile, it's a win.

Renovation Work Order: The Finish Work

The Beige Replacement: Go through your calendar for the upcoming week. Identify one social obligation or habit that feels like *obligatory beige*—something you do only because you've always done it. Delete it or replace it with thirty minutes of a color you actually enjoy.

The Trim Purchase: Physically go out and acquire one small item that serves as the *Crown Jewel* of your current space. Whether it's fresh flowers for the *Kitchen* or a high-quality coffee bean, put the *Trim* in place and notice how it changes the room's atmosphere.

The Private Build Log: Choose one new dream or project you're curious about and start a private note in your phone. For the next seven days, record your progress here instead of posting it on social media. This is your *Curing* process—letting the joy of the work belong solely to you.

Speak It Out Loud:

I am done living in beige. I am painting my life with joy, beauty, and purpose. I am not just a survivor; I am a masterpiece in progress, and I love the colors I'm choosing.

11

THE GUEST LIST

WHO GETS A KEY?

The paint is dry, the light fixtures are sparkling, and the house feels like you. It's a sanctuary, Sis. But here's what happens when you build something beautiful: people start knocking. Some are coming because they love you and want to celebrate your new space, but others are coming because they're looking for a place to drop their bags. It is time to talk about the guest list.

In your old house—the one with the rotted floors and the drafty windows—you didn't really have a guest list. You had an *Open-Door Policy* born out of a need to be liked or a fear of being alone. You let people track mud across your carpet and lean against your *Load-Bearing Lies* until the whole place felt heavy. But this new house has a different code. You've put too much sweat, tears, and *Sledgehammer Time* into these walls to let just anyone walk through them.

I. Managing the Guest List

Managing your *Guest List* isn't about being mean or exclusive; it's about stewardship. You are the steward of this peace. Not everyone who knew you in the *Demolition Phase* is qualified to live with you in the *Finished Phase*. Some people only know how to relate to you when you're a mess; they don't know what to do with a version of you that is whole and firm. You have to decide who gets a key, who gets an invitation, and who stays on the sidewalk.

There are three types of people on your list:

The Porch People: These are the acquaintances. You can be kind to them, you can wave from the window, and you can even have a chat on the steps. But they don't come inside. They haven't earned the right to see your *Rough-In* or sit at your table.

The Living Room Guests: These are the friends you enjoy. They respect the house rules. They don't track in mud. They can stay for a while, but they don't have a key. When the party is over, they go home, and you get your space back.

The Key-Holders: This is your *Inner Circle*. These are the few people who helped you carry the drywall and held the flashlight when the power went out. They didn't just show up for the housewarming; they were there when the pipes were leaking.

They love the house as much as you do. You trust them with the codes because they've proven they will help you protect the peace you've built.

If someone from your past keeps trying to kick the door down, remember: a *No* is a deadbolt. And it is a complete sentence. You don't owe an explanation for why your guest list has changed. Your house, your rules.

II. The House Rules: Shoes at the Door

Once you've decided who gets an invitation, you have to decide how they are expected to act once they step over the threshold. You've probably seen those cute, rustic signs in people's entryways that list the *House Rules*—"Always be kind," "We say sorry." Those are sweet, but we're talking about the kind of rules that protect your literal sanity.

In my house, one of the biggest rules is simple: *Leave your shoes at the door.* Why? Because I'm a busy woman. Let's be honest, I don't always have the time or the desire to sweep, mop, and vacuum every single day just because someone else was careless. I've worked too hard to get these floors clean and keep the rot out. I don't want the dust, the dirt, or the *Street Grime* from your life being dragged across my sanctuary.

Your life needs a *Shoe Rule*, too. When people come into

your space—whether it's a physical visit or just a long phone call—they are carrying the dirt of their own drama, their own negativity, and their own unhealed messes. If you let them walk right into your heart with those dirty shoes on, you are the one who has to clean up the mess after they leave. And if you aren't careful, that *Street Grime* will soak past your new rugs and start to rot your subfloor all over again.

The Policy: You are allowed to have standards for how people behave in your presence. You can say, "In this house, we don't do gossip," or "In this house, we don't raise our voices." It's your floor; you're the one who has to maintain it.

The Enforcement: If someone refuses to follow the rules after they've been warned, protect your peace by any means necessary! You can politely, firmly, and calmly show them to the door. You aren't kicking them out because you're angry; you're asking them to leave because they aren't respecting the maintenance of the home you've built.

III. Access Denied: The Inner Sanctum

Now, listen close, because this is where people get confused: Just because someone has been invited into the *Living Room*, or maybe even has a key to the front door, does not mean they have the right to go into your bedroom or go rummaging through your personal belongings. When people overstep their bounds, you have every right—honey, you had better—let them know where things stand.

When I was a child in my parents' home, they had every right to access my belongings. But baby, let my momma try to do that now? No ma'am! Your access to my *Inner Sanctum* has been denied! This is my bedroom, and you have no place in it.

The Boundary: Boundaries change over time, and it is your job to maintain them.

The Stance: For a person who chooses to disrespect or overstep their place in your life, let them know with all the love and sweetness you can muster—and hold your ground!

You have worked too hard—and I know, because I've been here with you this whole time—you have worked too hard to go back to where you were. You are the gatekeeper of this home. You choose who enters, you set the terms of your time, and you protect the *Master Suite* of your heart with everything you've got.

Just because we built an *Open Concept Life* doesn't mean you're living in a studio apartment where everyone gets to see your unmade bed the moment they walk in the front door. You've framed out specific rooms for a reason. The transparency we built in Chapter 6 is for your growth, not an intruder's curiosity.

Applying Your Site Rules

1. **The Domino Move: Stewardship.** Pick one person who has been acting like a *Key-Holder* but treating your house like a dumpster and move them to the *Porch*. You aren't hiding the view; you're revoking the entry code.

2. **Build the Fence, Not the Willpower: The Shoe Rule.** Instead of using willpower to not be bothered by someone's negativity, build a fence by setting the standard before they enter the room. If someone starts rummaging through your life, use your *Polite Deadbolt*: "I love you, but that part of my life isn't open for discussion right now."

3. **Keep the Scoreboard: Access and Authority.** Did you say *No* to an uninvited guest today? Did you enforce a *House Rule* without offering a 20-minute explanation? Record that as a win.

Renovation Work Order: The Stewardship Audit

The Key Audit: Make a list of your *Inner Circle*. Ask yourself: If my life were a construction site today, are these the people who would hold the flashlight, or are they the ones who would just complain about the dust? If they haven't earned the code, move them to the *Living Room* list.

Enforce the Shoe Rule: Identify one "dirty" conversation topic—gossip, old drama, or negativity—that someone always tracks into your house. The next time they start, politely say: "I'm working hard to keep the air clean in my new space, so I'm not talking about that anymore."

Lock the Inner Sanctum: Identify one area of your life (finances, marriage, past trauma) that you have been allowing *Living Room Guests* to rummage through. Install the deadbolt today. Stop offering the tour. Your *Master Suite* is private for a reason.

Speak It Out Loud:

Access to me is a privilege, not a right. I set the rules, I hold the keys, and I will not go back to the mess I left behind. This is my sanctuary, and it stays clean.

12

HOME MAINTENANCE

THE DAILY SWEEP

Look at this house! It's beautiful, it's solid, and it smells like fresh paint and peace. You did it, Sis. You really did. But let me tell you a secret that the makeover shows don't always show you: the day the contractor leaves is the day the maintenance starts. You can't just lock the door and hope it stays this way. You have to live in it, and living means upkeep.

A lot of us have renovated our lives before, only to find ourselves back in a mess six months later. We wonder what happened. Did the walls fail? No. We just stopped doing the *Daily Sweep*. Maintenance isn't about doing a *Gut Job* every day; it's about the small, consistent habits that keep the rot from ever coming back. We are shifting from the major renovation job of the mindset reset to the lifestyle of *Residency*. We are keeping house.

I. The Daily Chores: The Spirit of the Morning

In a home, if you don't do the dishes, the kitchen starts to smell. In your new life, your daily chores are the small habits that prevent emotional clutter from piling up.

The Morning Walk-Through: Every morning, before the world starts calling your name, check the *Internal Climate* of your home. Are you feeling a draft of anxiety? Is there a leak of resentment dripping in the corner? Spend five minutes checking your *Pillars*. Are you standing square? If the foundation of your peace feels a little tilted, you need to adjust your *Shims. Shims* are those small, vital wedges used to level a house—for you, that might be a moment of focused breath, a cup of coffee in silence, or reciting your truth. It's easier to tighten a faucet than it is to replace a flooded basement.

The Evening Dish-Wash: Every evening, sweep your mind of the day's grime. Let's be real: life happens. Traffic may have made you late, or you got a piece of bad news. It just is what it is. But you have to make a conscious choice to stabilize your climate and release those stressors so you can sleep peacefully. Write down three things that tracked dirt into your day and decide to leave them at the door. Don't let today's mess sit in the sink overnight.

II. The Weekly Chores: Clearing the Filters

Every week, you have to service the systems that allow you to breathe. If you don't change your HVAC filters, the air gets heavy and the system works twice as hard.

Mental Airflow: The world is constantly throwing dust at you—other people's opinions and social media noise. If you don't have a practice of clearing the air through silence or gratitude, your internal atmosphere gets heavy.

The Filter Change: Identify one dusty source of information (an app, a certain news cycle, a negative friend) and change the filter. Take a break from it for 48 hours and see how much better you can breathe.

III. The Seasonal Reset: Adjusting the Major Systems

Every few months, a smart homeowner does a deep check. Maintenance means being honest enough to say, "This system worked for me last year, but I've outgrown it." You are allowed to upgrade your appliances and your boundaries as you grow.

The Lock Audit: Just because someone had a key last season doesn't mean the level of their access hasn't shifted. Think of it like a *Smart Lock*—you can change the code whenever the season of the relationship changes. Conflict doesn't have to arrive in order to cause a shift. Like a seasonal change of clothes, some relationships are for a season of *Construction* but don't fit your season of *Residency*.

The Goal Alignment: Think back over your last 90 days. Have your goals or needs changed? Have you found yourself back in a place of saying "yes" to everyone even though their needs do not suit yours? Take a mental note of where the system is lagging, decide on the best course of action, and get started!

IV. Your Atmospheric Spring Cleaning: Moving the Furniture

Every few months, a smart homeowner doesn't just tidy up; they do a deep dive. They wash the baseboards and declutter that *Catch-All Table* where everyone throws their stuff.

Under the Rug: In your life, furniture represents your long-standing habits and comforts. Every 90 days, ask yourself: Is this routine still serving me, or is it just covering up a stain on the carpet?

The Catch-All Table: We all have that one spot where the junk of life accumulates—mental piles of tasks you're avoiding. Clear it off. If it doesn't belong in your new season, it doesn't get to stay on the table.

The Fresh Air Reset: Be intentional about taking time for yourself to truly rest. Just having that seasonal, consistent reset allows you to notice the maintenance needs before they become emergencies.

V. Curb Appeal: The Porch and the World

Finally, keep an eye on your *Curb Appeal*. This isn't about what other people think; it's about how you feel when you pull into your own driveway. If you let bitterness or busyness grow like weeds around your front door, it becomes harder to get inside to your peace.

The Curb Appeal Audit: Stand on your virtual sidewalk and ask yourself:

What am I advertising to the street? When people look at your life right now, do they see a "Welcome" mat or a "Beware of Dog" sign? If you are constantly projecting defensiveness, you might be attracting the very chaos you're trying to avoid.

Are the weeds of Busyness blocking the door? Have you let your schedule get so overgrown with "yeses" that you can't even find the path to your own front door?

Is the porch light on? Kindness and gratitude are the lighting of your life. Is your light still shining, or has bitterness unscrewed the bulb?

Is the House Rules sign still legible? Can people see your boundaries before they even knock? Or have you let your rules get weathered and faded?

Applying Your Site Rules

1. **The Domino Move: Calibration.** Now that the house is built, the goal shifts to calibration. Use your morning coffee to check the level of your peace. If you feel a **shift in your internal climate**, adjust your *Shims* (truth statements) before you open the front door.

2. **Build the Fence, Not the Willpower: Schedule the Inspection.** Instead of using willpower to remember to check your boundaries, build a fence by scheduling your *Spring Cleaning* resets on your calendar. Let the routine protect you.

3. **Keep the Scoreboard: Propulsion over Stagnation.** Did you move the furniture and address a hidden habit today? Did you acknowledge a change in access for a guest without a fight? Record that as a win.

Renovation Work Order: The Master Maintenance Manual

The Shim Session: Perform a structural level-check of your *Internal Climate* every morning. Identify one area where your peace feels tilted or your confidence is sagging. Drive a *shim* into that spot by speaking a non-negotiable truth out loud (e.g., My No is a deadbolt). Repeat the statement until you feel the structural shift and the door stops sticking.

The Filter Purge: Identify the #1 digital or social source that tracks *dust* into your mental airflow—the app or news cycle that leaves you feeling drained and annoyed. Perform a 48-hour offload this weekend. Notice the shift in your *Internal Climate* when the intake valve is closed. If the air is cleaner without the noise, make the filter change permanent.

The Key Collection: Audit your recent messages for a guest who has been rummaging through your *Inner Sanctum* without an invite. Instead of a confrontation, simply re-key the lock. The next time they bring a fire to your door, use the *Intercom Script*: That sounds like a lot to handle. I don't have the square footage for that topic today, but I'd love to hear about [Neutral Topic].

The Curb Appeal Walk-Through: Stand on your *virtual sidewalk* and audit your last five outgoing texts or social posts. Read them as if you were a stranger. If you see the weeds of bitterness or the grime of busyness blocking the path, pull them. Delete one negative post or send one gratitude text to a faithful few who respects your home. Turn your *Porch Light* back on.

Speak It Out Loud:

I am a Master Homeowner. I am not just a survivor; I am a maintainer of peace. I catch the leaks early, I keep my soul clear, and I am not going back to the rot. This house is my sanctuary, and it is here to stay.

13

FINAL ACCEPTANCE

HANDING OVER THE KEYS

Whew! Sis, come here and sit down for a minute. Leave the broom in the corner. Look at this place—can you believe we actually did it? We've rolled up the blueprints. The tools have been put away, and the dust from the renovation has finally settled. The work is done.

Take a look around. This was no small feat. When we first sat down with those blueprints, this house was just a collection of drafty rooms and load-bearing lies. You didn't just put a fresh coat of paint on a crumbling structure; you did the heavy lifting. You spent weeks in the trenches. You tore out the rot, you reinforced the foundation, and you survived the demolition days when it felt like the dust would never settle.

A renovation like this doesn't happen in a weekend makeover show—it took time, it took grit, and it took a willingness to stay in the mess until the beauty emerged. You've traded your old, shaky shell for a sanctuary that is solid, leveled, and uniquely yours. You aren't just looking at a blueprint anymore—you are standing in your life.

This is your housewarming. I want you to take a long, deep breath. Can you feel the difference? The air is clearer. The ground is firmer. The draft that used to keep you shivering at night is gone because you've insulated your peace.

II. The Contractor is Moving Out

But as we wrap this up, I want to tell you the most important thing of all: The contractor isn't moving into this house—YOU are. I've been here to help you hold the level and swing the hammer, but these are your keys. This is your deed. You are no longer a guest in someone else's expectations. You are the Proprietor of your own soul.

When I say the Contractor isn't moving in, I'm talking about the consultants in your life. Other Contractors might be your therapist, your pastor, your best friend, or even that voice of authority you've always listened to—really, it's anyone whose voice has been louder than your own during this build. Throughout this book, I've been acting as your lead Contractor. I've been the one holding the blueprints and suggesting the layout, but the Contractor doesn't have to live with the results.

The Contractor gets to leave at 5:00 PM: We all go back to our own houses. We don't have to deal with the leaky faucet of your difficult relationship or the drafty window of your late-night anxieties. You do.

The Contractor doesn't pay the mortgage: Since you are the one paying for this life with your time and energy, you are the only one who gets to decide if the design actually works for you.

The Contractor isn't the Boss of your Joy: If your soul is crying out for Vibrant Red, you'd better pick up the red brush! Only you truly know what is going to bring you joy, and honey, you have earned every stroke of that vibrancy.

I'm stepping off the property. My job was to help you find your own strength and style. Now, you're the owner. If you want to move the furniture over six inches to the right so that it catches the morning sun, move it. If you want to change the House Rules, change them. You are no longer building a life to pass an inspection from others; you are building a life that feels like home to YOU.

III. Living in the Finished Work

A house isn't meant to be a museum. It's meant to be lived in. There will be scuffs on the baseboards. There will be a spill on the rug. When that happens, I don't want you to think the house is ruined. No! Just go get the mop! You've built a structure that is strong enough to handle a little bit of "life." You know where the tools are now. You are no longer afraid of the repair process because you know you are worth the maintenance.

Your New Neighborhood

As you step out onto your new porch, you're going to notice that the world looks different. You'll start to see other women out there, swinging their own hammers. Support them. Share your tools. Supporting your neighbors doesn't mean you become their general contractor. You can hand them a wrench over the fence without walking onto their job site and getting covered in their dust. And never, ever let anyone talk you into tearing down what you've built to make them more comfortable. You bled for these floors. You cried for this ceiling—and that crown molding you chose is gorgeous! Hold your ground.

Not everyone is going to be happy with your glow-up. Expect it, maintain your boundary, and if they refuse to respect the new foundation you've laid, show them the door. Love them where they are, but love yourself enough to walk away so that you can fully embrace your new space.

IV. The Final Sit-Down: Just Between Us

We started this journey with a fresh pot of coffee and a messy blueprint. Now, the coffee is still warm, but the blueprint has become a reality. We aren't talking about "what if" anymore; we're sitting in "what is."

In this moment, I'm just basking in the version of you that is unapologetically you. As I look at you, I see you owning all the pieces that make you unique. You aren't hiding the work in progress anymore or waiting for someone else's permission to exist. You are standing tall, confident, wise, and steady. You've reclaimed your fearless self. You've secured your peace.

I know there were days when you looked at the rubble and thought, "I should have just stayed in the mess." I saw the sweat on your brow when we were tearing down those load-bearing lies, and I saw the fire in your eyes when you finally put that deadbolt on the Inner Sanctum. I am so incredibly proud of you.

As I get ready to head out, I want you to hear me. This house isn't just a structure; it's a testimony to your resilience. You've built a life that finally fits the woman you were intended to be. Don't let anyone—not even your own old thoughts—tell you that you don't deserve to sit in this peace. You paid for every square inch of this sanctuary with your growth, your grit, and the hard work that you put in. Thank you for trusting this process and trusting me to walk through it with you.

So, keep the coffee warm. Keep the House Rules firm. And every now and then, just sit here on this couch and listen to the quiet. That's the sound of a woman who is finally, truly, at home.

Give me a hug. I'm just a phone call away if you ever need to borrow a ladder, but honestly? I think you've got it from here.

Renovation Work Order: The Owner's Log

The Acceptance Audit: Record the moment you sat in your new sanctuary and felt like the true owner. Did you make a decision without asking for a Contractor's opinion? Your victory today isn't about a task you completed; it's about a space you occupied.

Calibrate the Climate: Perform a final check of your *Internal Climate*. Is the air still clear? If you feel a draft of old guilt trying to seep in, remind yourself that the Contractor has moved out. You are the only one who sets the thermostat now.

The Sovereign Soul Win: Identify one "design choice" you made in this build that was purely for your joy—not for your mom, your boss, or your neighbors. Acknowledge that you no longer need a permit to be happy.

Speak it Out Loud:

I am the owner of this space. I am worthy of this peace. I am capable of the upkeep. I am no longer defined by the rot of my past, but by the strength of my foundation. I am home.

V. The "New Address" Announcement

OFFICIAL CHANGE OF ADDRESS

NAME:

PREVIOUS RESIDENCE: The Corner of People-Pleasing and Survival Mode.

NEW RESIDENCE: The Sanctuary of Peace & Purpose.

PLEASE NOTE:

- My boundaries have been updated.

- My Inner Sanctum is now private.

- I am no longer accepting deliveries of drama, gossip, or old labels.

- If you'd like to visit, please remember the House Rules: Shoes (and negativity) at the door.

I've moved into the life I was always meant to live. It's taken some work, but the view is beautiful and the foundation is solid. I was never lost—I've just finally moved home.

14

The Owner's Manual: The Bonus Rooms

A Supplemental Guide for Living in Your New Build

You've built a masterpiece, Sis. The foundation is cured, the walls are up, and the keys are in your hand. But a house is more than a structure—it's the setting for your life. These *Bonus Rooms* are where the blueprint meets the real world. Think of this as your "Owner's Manual" for the specific areas of life that require a different kind of maintenance.

15

THE GARDEN

CULTIVATING STRATEGIC SYNERGY

Once the house is finished, you'll start to look out the windows at the lot around you. In your old life, you might have been a wildflower—growing wherever the wind blew you, often getting stepped on or choked out by thorns. But in this new season, you are a gardener.

This isn't just about being nice; it's about being strategic. We've already dispelled the lies that you aren't enough. You are now embracing your fullness unapologetically, and that means you are ready to fully accept your worth and the value that you bring to the table. We aren't looking for people to fix, and we aren't looking for people to fill us. We are looking for synergy—the idea that 1 + 1 equals more than 2. It's not about what you can take from someone else, but two whole people standing in the same soil, helping each other reach higher for the sun.

A garden doesn't just happen; it is designed. Strategic relationships are about synergy. It's about two whole people standing in the same soil, helping each other reach higher for the sun.

I. The Soil Test: Identifying Strategic Connections

Before you plant, you have to know what you're putting in the ground. You are looking for high-yield connections. These aren't just people you like; these are people who align with the new foundation you've built. Think of your garden as the curb appeal your neighbors see from the sidewalk, but only your Key-Holders from Chapter 11 get to come inside the gate and help you harvest the fruit.

Look for the Four A's:

1. **Alignment:** Do they value what you value? If you value peace and they thrive on drama, you're planting a cactus in a rainforest. It won't work.

2. **Ambition (Personal or Professional):** Are they also in a renovation phase? Strategic friends are those who are actively growing. They are the ones who don't just admire your Paint and Trim; they bring their own tools to the table. You want people who are reaching, not just resting.

3. **Accountability:** Will they tell you when your paint is peeling? A strategic friend loves you enough to hold the level and tell you if your boundaries are leaning.

4. **Ability to Reciprocate:** Synergy requires two-way watering. If you are always the one with the watering can and they never bring the fertilizer, that's a parasite, not a partner.

II. The Cross-Pollination Effect

Synergy is about complementary strengths. In a real garden, different plants help each other—some provide shade, some fix nitrogen in the soil, and some ward off pests. Strategic synergy looks like this:

- **The Visionary & The Builder:** You have the big idea; they know how to lay the bricks.

- **The Encourager & The Challenger:** You provide the warmth; they provide the iron sharpening push to be better.

- **The Safe Harbor & The North Star:** One friend is where you go when you're tired; the other is who you call when you've lost your way.

When you find these people, you don't just hang out. You collaborate on life. You share resources, you vet each other's ideas, and you celebrate each other's Grand Openings as if they were your own.

III. The Deep Probe: Garden Inspection

- **The Nitrogen Check:** Who in your life makes you feel more capable of achieving your goals after you spend time with them? That is your nitrogen.

- **The Shade Test:** Do you have friends who overshadow your growth—constantly making the conversation about them—or do they provide the protective shade you need to bloom at your own pace?

- **The Transactional Trap:** Are you choosing friends based on what they can do for your status, or what they do for your soul?

Practical Application: Cultivating the Crop

The Seed Swap Initiative: Identify one person you admire for a specific growth trait (e.g., their discipline, their peace, their business savvy). Reach out and say: *"I really admire how you handle [Trait]. I'm working on that in my own life. I'd love to grab coffee and hear your perspective—and I'd love to share some of what I'm learning about [Your Strength] if that would be helpful to you."*

The Weed and Feed Audit: Look at your top 5 closest connections.

Weed: If a relationship is based solely on commiserating (bonding over complaining), it's a weed. Stop watering the complaints.

Feed: Choose one High-Yield friend and intentionally feed that relationship this week by sending them a resource, a lead, or a word of encouragement that specifically helps their build.

Speak It Out Loud:

I am a master gardener of my connections. I do not settle for wildflowers that choke my peace. I intentionally plant seeds of synergy, and I nurture relationships where we both grow taller, stronger, and more vibrant because we stand together.

16

THE HOME OFFICE

PURPOSE AND CAREER

This is the boss move of the book. We've already done the internal demolition—we've torn down the *I'm not enough* walls and the *I'm lucky to be here* flooring. Now, we are stepping into the Home Office not as a tenant, but as the proprietor. You aren't trying to earn your seat at the table anymore; you realized you *own* the table. You're just deciding if this office has the right lighting for your vision.

In this room, we aren't asking for permission to exist; we are presenting the invoice for the value we provide. You are the CEO of your future, and it is time to align your paycheck and your position with the powerhouse woman you've become.

For a long time, you might have been working in a cubicle of someone else's making—squeezing your personality, your time, and your gifts into a role that was three sizes too small. You stayed there because the Load-Bearing Lies told you that you should just be grateful to have a seat at the table. But we've already dispelled those lies. We've cleared the rot of imposter syndrome and hauled away the *not enough* debris. You are now standing in the fullness of yourself, unapologetically. When you walk into your workspace now, you aren't looking for validation; you are bringing value.

I. The Desk Height: Aligning Your Work with Your Worth

In the Home Office, we adjust the desk to fit you. If you have spent months renovating your *Internal Climate* to be a woman of peace and power, you cannot spend 40 hours a week in a role that treats you like a handyman for everyone else's emergencies.

The Gifts Assessment: Take a look at your hands. What are the unique tools you bring to your work? Maybe it's your strategic eye, your ability to calm a chaotic room, or your technical mastery. In your old life, you downplayed these gifts. In this new life, these are your *billable assets.*

II. Bringing the Receipts: The Audit of Success

You wouldn't pay a contractor for a renovation without seeing the finished work, right? The same applies to you. If you are sitting at that desk wondering if you deserve a raise or a promotion, it's time to check the project logs.

The Receipt File: Start a literal folder (digital or physical) called the *Receipts*. Every time you solve a problem, save the company money, lead a team through a crisis, or get a glowing review, put it in the file.

The Market Value Check: If you've renovated your skills but you're still getting paid pre-renovation wages, there is a leak in your bank account that needs to be plugged. Do you have your receipts ready to lay on the table? Can you say, *"Based on the structure I've built here and the value I've added, my compensation needs to reflect the current market value of my expertise"*?

III. The Deep Probe: What's Blocking the Door?

Is it Fear or the Floor? Are you afraid of the new role, or are you just used to the creaky floorboards of your current comfort zone?

The Promotion of Treatment: Sometimes the position we need to pursue isn't a new title, but a new standard of how we are treated. What is holding you back from demanding a workspace that is free of toxic rot?

Practical Application: The CEO Shift

The Invoice Exercise: Tonight, sit at your desk and write out a formal invoice to your current employer or your career path. List five major renovations you've successfully led in your role over the last year. Attach a price tag to them—how much time, energy, and revenue did you save them? Look at that total. **That is your leverage.**

The New Position Sketch: If you were the Architect of your perfect workday, what would the layout look like?

- What time does the office door close?

- What kind of coworkers are allowed in the room?

- What is the salary ceiling you are ready to break through?

The Assignment: Identify one step (a certification, a conversation, a resume update) that gets you closer to that shift.

Speak It Out Loud:

I am the proprietor of my talent and the CEO of my time. I do not settle for pre-renovation wages for a post-renovation woman. My value is non-negotiable, my receipts are ready, and I am the only one who determines the height of my desk.

17

THE FAMILY ROOM

MARRIAGE AND PARENTING

Welcome to the *Family Room*. If the kitchen is the heart of the home, this room is the lungs—the place with the big sectional couch where everyone gathers. But here's the thing about shared spaces: it's a lot harder to keep the floors clean when other people are living on them. In this room, your renovation meets reality.

Sis, we have to get real for a second, because the *Family Room* is usually where even the best renovations go to die. We spend all this time doing the deep internal work—tearing down the lies and building up our worth—but then we walk through our own front door and immediately shrink back into the Chief-of-Everything. We've spent this whole book learning how to stand tall, yet the minute we hit the living room, we have a habit of laying back down like a human doormat.

If you are carrying the entire mental and physical load for every person in that house, you aren't a homemaker—you're a mule. And let's be honest, a tired mule eventually kicks. That explosive feeling you get when you see one more dish in the sink, or that tension where your family feels like they're walking on eggshells around you? That is the sound of a woman whose structure is under way too much pressure. It's the sound of a foundation that wasn't meant to carry everyone else's weight alone. You've worked too hard to build this home to turn it into a stable.

If you've been the fixer, the do-it-all, or the silent sufferer for years, your spouse and your kids are used to the old layout. When you suddenly put up a load-bearing boundary or refuse to let them track mud into your peace, they might get confused. They might even try to re-decorate back to the old way. Your job in this room isn't to renovate them—it's to maintain your new standards while leading them into a healthier way of living together.

I. The Spouse Suite: Renovating the Partnership

In marriage, it's easy to let the paint peel over time. You get busy, you get tired, and you start treating your partner like a roommate or, worse, a project.

The Foundation Check: Is your marriage built on mutual respect, or is it leaning on one person doing all the emotional heavy lifting?

Updating the Layout: If you have changed, your marriage must change. You have to communicate the new House Rules. You might say, *"I love you, but I can't be the only one cleaning up the emotional messes in this house anymore. I need us to build this together."* A healthy partner will appreciate the new strength in the house; a toxic one will miss the old, easy version of you. Hold your ground.

II. The Kids' Wing: Building for the Next Generation

Parenting is the ultimate legacy build. The house you build for yourself today is the model home your children will use to build their own lives tomorrow.

Lead by Design: If you want your children to have boundaries, they need to see you have them. When you say, *"Mommy needs 20 minutes of quiet time to recharge,"* you aren't being selfish; you're teaching them how to insulate their own souls.

Clearing the Inheritance: We all inherit junk from our own parents—old ways of arguing, hidden shames, or leaky habits. Your job is to make sure that junk stops with you. You are the filter. You make sure that the air in the kids' wing is cleaner than the air you grew up breathing.

III. Shared Maintenance: Relinquishing the Broom

In this room, we have to talk about balance, accountability, and the broom. We've already established your worth and built your boundaries. Now, we have to see if those boundaries actually hold up.

The Control Leak: Control is often just a mask for anxiety. We think if we do it all, it will be perfect. But perfection is a cold, lonely house.

The Flawed Finish: You have to allow for a flawed finish. If your husband loads the dishwasher wrong, but the dishes are getting done, leave the kitchen! If your kids' beds are lumpy, but they made them themselves, tell them, *"Good job,"* and close the door. You have to relinquish enough control to allow them to be stakeholders in the home.

IV. Training the Crew: The Site Meeting

You cannot be the only one who knows where the cleaning supplies are. Sit the crew down. Hand out the blueprints. Say, *"I have done the work to embrace a life of peace, and that means I am no longer the sole Maintenance Department for this family. I need us to build this together."*

If you don't teach your children to fend for themselves, you aren't loving them—you're sending them out into the world with a shaky foundation. Let them struggle with the broom. You are building their resilience while protecting your own *Internal Climate.*

V. From Museum to Home

If the House Rules are so rigid that nobody can laugh, you haven't built a sanctuary; you've built a museum.

The Laughter Insulation: Joy is the best insulation for a home. It keeps the warmth in and the bitterness out.

The Memory Lot: What do you want your children to remember? The perfectly folded towels, or the night you ordered pizza and had a dance party in the living room? Keep the house clean, yes, but keep the Internal Climate light.

Practical Application: The Shared Space Audit

The Load-Bearing Check: Identify one area in your marriage or parenting where you've been over-functioning. Today, step back and let that person manage their own square foot of the house.

The Drop the Broom Challenge: This week, identify one task you normally snatch back because it isn't being done "just right." Let them do it. Even if it's only 70% as good as yours, celebrate the 70% and keep your hands in your pockets.

The Site Meeting: Schedule a formal check-in with your crew. Hand out the updated House Rules and clearly define the new maintenance schedule. Stop offering the tour of your emotional labor; start delegating the upkeep.

The Legacy Question: Ask yourself: *"If my child built a house exactly like the one I'm living in right now, would I be happy for them?"* If the answer is no, identify the specific "room" that needs a standard-shift today.

Speak It Out Loud:

I am the Matriarch of this home. My peace is contagious, and my boundaries are a blessing to my family. We are building a legacy of health, one brick and one conversation at a time. I am not a mule; I am the heart of a balanced and joyful home.

18

THE STORM SHELTER

DEALING WITH DISAPPOINTMENT

This is the final room of the manual—the one we hope stays empty, but the one that proves the worth of everything you've built. Because let's face it: life doesn't care how nice your new crown molding is when a hurricane is coming. This room is about resilience. It's the difference between a house that looks good in the sun and a house that stands through the flood.

The storm shelter isn't a separate building; it's the part of your foundation that was poured deepest. When the wind howls, you don't have to be strong—you just have to sit in the strength of what you've already built.

You can build the most beautiful, up-to-code life in the world, but you cannot control the weather. Disappointment is like a sudden hailstorm. You did everything right—you cleared the rot, you poured the foundation, you painted the walls—and then, out of nowhere, a storm hits. A job is lost. A health report comes back scary. A person you trusted walks out the door.

When that happens, the first thing we usually do is blame the house. We think, *"I must have built it wrong,"* or *"I guess this new life thing doesn't work."* But honey, hear me: The storm isn't proof that your house is bad; the fact that you're still standing is proof that your house is strong.

I. The Deep Probe: Structural Integrity

The Blueprint Check: When something goes wrong, is your first instinct to blame your worth or the situation?

The Insurance Claim: Are you allowing grace to cover the scuffs on your exterior, or are you letting the damage become your identity?

II. Practical Application: Weathering the Season

The 24-Hour Shelter Rule: When a major setback hits, give yourself a 24-hour Shelter Pass. For one day, you don't have to fix it or be strong. Your only job is to stay in the shelter and breathe. Do not attempt to repair the roof while the lightning is still striking.

Stock the Shelter: Identify three Non-Negotiable Truths that the storm cannot touch. These are your emergency supplies for your soul.

- *I am still worthy of peace.*

- *I still have my foundation.*

- *This storm is temporary.*

The Post-Storm Inspection: Once the clouds clear, don't just mourn the debris. Walk the perimeter. What parts of your structure held up perfectly? What boundaries stood firm? Use the damage as a guide for where you might need to reinforce your next build.

Practical Application: The Resilience Audit

The Shelter Inventory: Write down your three Non-Negotiable Truths today, while the sun is shining. Place them in a digital vault or a physical notebook. You need to know where the flashlights are before the power goes out.

Identify the Draft: Is there a window in your life that always rattles when the wind blows—a specific insecurity or a toxic person? Install the weather-stripping today. Decide what truth or boundary will act as the seal against that specific draft.

The Grace Clause: Look at a recent scuff or mistake in your life. Instead of trying to sand it down immediately, apply the Insurance Claim. Remind yourself: *The structure is sound; the finish is just being tested.*

Speak It Out Loud:

I am not afraid of the clouds. My house is built on a rock, and I have a shelter for the rain. The storm may hit my walls, but it cannot touch my soul. I am safe, I am covered, and I will still be standing when the sun comes up.

THE AUTHOR'S NOTE

SAYING THE QUIET PART OUT LOUD

Before I let you go, I want to say the quiet part out loud.

If you haven't picked up on it throughout this book, I am a praying Christian woman—unapologetically. I wrote this book because I needed it for myself, but also because of a vital truth I realized in my own seasons of construction: truth doesn't need a sermon to change you.

I. The Method: Coffee Table Conversations

When I was in the middle of my rubble, fighting for my peace, I didn't need a lecture; I needed a sister—someone who could hear my cries and even sometimes my cusses, overlook them, and meet me at the point of my need. I realized that sometimes, our approach can become a barrier to the very healing it's meant to provide. God calls for us to carry out the instructions He has given to us—and that requires making those instructions plain and actionable. Everything in these pages is built on the rock-solid foundation of the Master Architect's original blue-prints—sound biblical wisdom.

II. The Work: Living the Blueprint Daily

I simply chose to deliver it in the language of the coffee table rather than the pulpit, because while the renovation begins at the feet of Jesus, it has to be lived out in the hallways of your life daily. You are responsible for carrying out your newfound freedom Monday through Saturday. This is where the transformation is practiced and eventually sticks.

Because we've been honest enough to do that work, we can now address the things that truly hold us back. I remember taking a shower one day and just telling God how I was feeling and asking why I couldn't seem to shake the sickness I had been dealing with. He clearly spoke to me and said: *You're sick because you're tired. You're tired because you're fighting because you have accepted words that I haven't spoken over you.*

I am calling you to a higher standard, Sis—right now. I need you to come out of agreement with words that have been spoken over you that do not align with God's assessment of your structure.

You don't have to waste another minute of your life fighting against load-bearing lies that eventually become self-fulfilling prophecies. At some point, you have to make a choice: Either God is true and the blueprints He has drawn for you must come to pass, or you believe Him to be a liar. If God didn't speak it over you, it's a lie! It is a defect in the material that does not belong in your build.

I want you to expel the lies you've been holding—the ones that don't match the Master Architect's original design. Stop trying so hard to fight them that you end up accidentally fulfilling them. There is something about just *being*—standing in the finished work of who you were intended to be—that is beautiful, pure, and empowering.

You aren't a project in need of a constant fix. You are a completed structure. When you stop struggling against the lies and simply occupy your space, the atmosphere changes. You don't have to prove your worth; you just have to reside in it.

III. The Commission: Fix Your Crown and Get to Stepping

Your perceived deficits do not define you; they are not limiting factors— they are the keys to unlocking your God-given superpowers. If God is your source, then why do you keep freaking out when there seems to be more month than money? If God has made you the head, then why do you accept and allow people to treat you like dirt?

Girl! Hold your head up high. Do you know who you are? Fix your crown and get to stepping. Honey, you are one baaaaddd mama jamma because the Great One lives on the inside of you. You are royalty. Your words hold power. There is no fight besides the fight to understand who God created you to be. Fight for that! Fight to be the most authentic, amazing, unstoppable, creative, solution-bearing, purpose-driven version of you!

IV. The Partnership: A Final Prayer

So now that you and I have both snotted, cried, and began the work on ourselves, let me remind you: God began the good work; now partner with Him because He is faithful to complete it. If you'll allow me, I'd love to leave you with a prayer of blessing over your new home:

Dear God,

I thank you for my sister who took the time to trust me with her heart. I pray that you heal every void and every broken place—yes, she has taken the time to do the work, but God, only You can fully fix what is broken. So today, we give ourselves to You completely—our past, our present, and our future.

As we tear down and rebuild, thank you for this beautiful life that You have given. We ask that you give her the wisdom and the strategy to use it for Your Glory and to walk boldly in the beauty and wonder that is everything that You have created her to be. Give her an unshakable confidence in what You can do through her so she is truly unstoppable. Help her not only to become the best version of herself—the one You originally created—but to also share that version, and the process, with someone else.

We pray these things, confident that You have heard us and that You will heal us.

In Jesus' Name, Amen!

The Blueprint Sources

References & Inspirations

A house is only as strong as the wisdom it's built on. While this book was written from the heart, the materials used to build these chapters were sourced from timeless truths, psychological foundations, and the collective wisdom of those who have mastered the art of living well.

When you know your materials are high-grade, you don't have to worry about the inspection. You aren't just winging it; you are building on Truth that has stood for thousands of years.

I. The Primary Foundation: Ancient Wisdom & Biblical Values

While this book is written to be accessible to every woman, the Architecture is heavily influenced by the Wisdom Literature of the Bible. These principles have served as the primary load-bearing beams for this build:

The Concept of the Rock (Matthew 7): The core necessity of building on a solid foundation rather than shifting sand.

The Principle of Stewardship: The firm belief that our lives, bodies, and spirits are a property we are tasked to manage and protect, not assets we are required to exhaust for others.

The Law of the Harvest (Galatians 6): The Garden concept—the truth that we eventually reap the peace or the chaos that we choose to plant and water.

The Sanctity of the Inner Room (Matthew 6): The value of the Inner Sanctum and the importance of private, internal work over public performance.

II. The Structural Design: Psychological Principles

To ensure the renovation was safe and sustainable, we utilized several key concepts from modern behavioral science and psychology:

Boundaries (Cloud & Townsend): The framework for the Guest List and House Rules, emphasizing that No is a tool for protection, not a weapon of offense.

Atomic Habits (James Clear): The Domino Move and Building the Fence—the science of using environmental design rather than willpower to sustain change.

Cognitive Reframing: The Demolition of Load-Bearing Lies, which mirrors the psychological process of identifying and replacing maladaptive thought patterns.

The Polyvagal Theory: The Wiring and Electrical section, focusing on how the nervous system regulates our internal temperature and response to stress.

III. The Material Sources: Real-Life Renovation

The analogies throughout this book are inspired by the universal language of home stewardship and construction:

The Gut Job Methodology: Based on the reality that superficial fixes—the paint job—never solve structural rot.

Maintenance Logs: Inspired by the high-performance habit of Daily Audits used in both project management and personal growth to ensure a life stays up to code.

This book was built to be a living document. The sources listed above are the stores where I've gathered and vetted my tools over the years. I encourage you to keep exploring these warehouses of wisdom as you continue to maintain your home.

Wisdom builds the house, but understanding establishes it; and by knowledge, the rooms are filled with all precious and pleasant riches. — Proverbs 24:3-4

ACKNOWLEDGEMENTS

I did not build this alone. This book was framed by the prayers, coffee conversations, and resoluteness of those who refused to let me stay in the midst of my rubble.

To the Original Architect: Thank You for the design of my heart. May I fulfill my purpose on this earth and bring You glory in every room I build.

To my Mother: Thank you for the fierce reminders of who I am and, more importantly, whose I am.

To the Women Who Surround Me: Thank you for always making room at your table and keeping honesty on your tongue.

To the Men Who Raised Me: I was your princess first. Thank you for speaking life to the woman within me and giving me the courage and the example to never forget my crown.

To my Sisters: Thank you for being just a phone call or a drive away. Thank you for the grace to sit with me in the ruins and the strength to never let me stay there. Your encouragement fueled me, but your confrontation gave me the courage to move forward.

To my Husband: Thank you for the grace and the space to renovate my life. Thank you for being the one who held the umbrella while I worked on the roof—for protecting me so I could focus on the build. I am a better woman because you gave me the room and the push to find myself again.

A Note from Lesley

Thank you for allowing me to share this space with you.

We began this journey as a conversation between friends over coffee, laying out the blueprints for a life of internal governance and structural peace. My hope is that these pages have provided you with the clarity needed to inspect your own "foundation" and begin the work of building a lasting legacy.

As an independent author and the founder of WP Press, I rely on the voices of my readers to help others find this work. If these conversations resonated with you, would you take a moment to leave an honest review on Amazon?

Reviews are the "social proof" that signal to other leaders and seekers that these blueprints are worth their time. Your feedback helps ensure that the message of the Sovereign Soul reaches those who are ready to move from chaos to intentional self-governance.

I am grateful for your time, your trust, and your commitment to the "hard hat" work of personal restoration.

With gratitude,

Lesley

Author & Strategist

Visit my Amazon Page

Continue the Conversation

Let's keep the conversation going! Join the WP community for more blueprints on structure, peace, and walking in the totality of your wealth at **mywealthpower.com**

The Next Build

Coming Soon from WP Press

R ebuilding your house was just Phase 1.

Let's keep the momentum going—we're talking about legacy—but it starts with understanding infrastructure and inheritance.

Most of us have been taught to manage lack, but few have been taught how to govern our inheritance. We've been living in a "Pauper Mindset"—that low-grade hum of functional anxiety and "not enough"—while the Father has been waiting for us at still waters with updated instructions.

If you enjoyed this book, we're just getting started. Get ready to jump into a new conversation soon!

The Power to Get Wealth

This isn't just about money; it's a treatise on purpose and a holistic definition of wealth. It is the overflow of your **Mind, Body, Spirit, and Soul**. In this next build, we explore:

- **The Internal Plumbing:** Why your life and business cannot expand beyond what your soul is structured to handle.

- **The Next Gen Shift:** Moving from individual monuments to "Legacy Architecture"—building the floors for the next generation.

- **The School of Hard Knocks:** Refining your greatest tests into the jewels of your legacy.

The Wealth Audit: What's in Your Hand?

The miracle is in the house. You've heard the knock. You've felt the debt of being undervalued. But the oil doesn't stop flowing until you run out of vessels.

Through **The Wealth Audit**, we provide the infrastructure for the **Sovereign Owner**—a place where raw talent is refined into high-value equity. It all comes down to you fully acknowledging the goldmine that has always been in your hand.

Are you ready to say yes?

About the Author

Lesley Morgan Jenkins has been dishing out her own special brand of spice since she was young, but today, she is mastering the refined art of seasoning. For years, Lesley operated as a professional "Organizational Chaos Tamer," stepping into nascent and struggling systems to build legacies through structure and efficiency. With a career spanning healthcare administration and nonprofit management, she spent decades navigating the complexities of operational excellence.

When the walls of her own life began to show cracks, Lesley reached a pivotal realization: you cannot build a brand well when you have not first learned to govern yourself. She discovered that no amount of business strategy could fix a compromised personal foundation, and that a woman's greatest legacy isn't her business—it's her peace.

In *Sovereign Soul Conversations*, Lesley moves her expertise from the boardroom to the interior. She bridges the gap between strategic leadership and personal sovereignty, teaching women that self-governance is the ultimate boss move. By clearing away social debris, she helps readers build a reality that is structurally sound and uniquely their own.

Today, Lesley is redefining what it means to live on her own terms as a wife, mother, and entrepreneur. She still brings the heat, but she's learning to apply it with the wisdom of a master builder who no longer seeks a permit to exist. She lives in the Metropolitan Atlanta area, maintaining a home built on the pillars of light, love, and laughter with her husband and two sons.

www.ingramcontent.com/pod-product-compliance
Lightning Source LLC
Chambersburg PA
CBHW071322150726
47997CB00002B/575